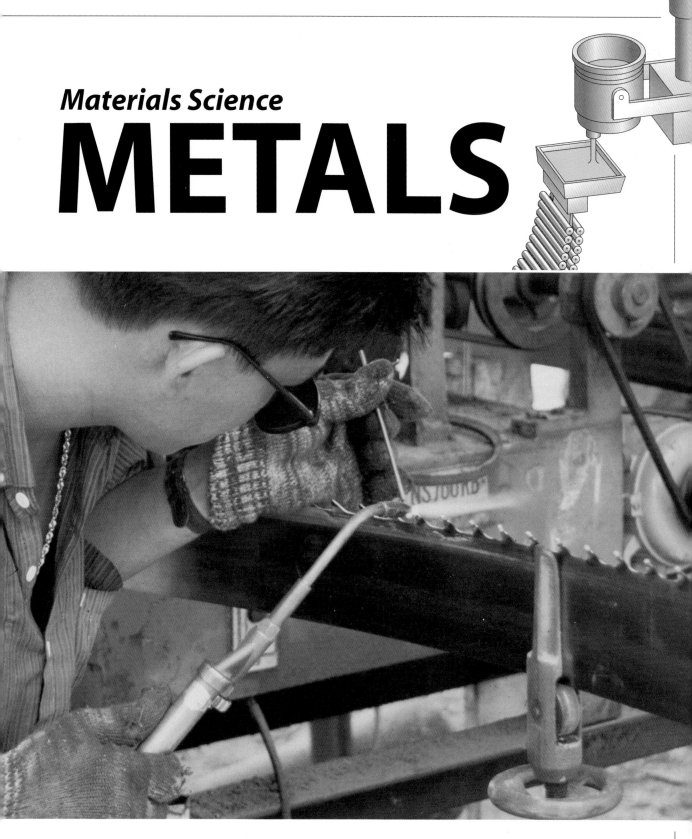

Materials Science
METALS

making use of the secrets of matter

✦ Atlantic Europe Publishing

First published in 2003 by
Atlantic Europe Publishing Company Ltd.

Copyright © 2003
Atlantic Europe Publishing Company Ltd.

Reprinted in 2005

Author
Brian Knapp, BSc, PhD

Art Director
Duncan McCrae, BSc

Senior Designer
Adele Humphries, BA, PGCE

Editors
Mary Sanders, BSc, and Gillian Gatehouse

Illustrations
David Woodroffe

Design and production
EARTHSCAPE EDITIONS

Scanning and retouching
Global Graphics sro, Czech Republic

Print
WKT Company Ltd., China

Materials Science – Volume 2: Metals
A CIP record for this book is available from the British Library

ISBN 1 86214 316 1

Acknowledgments
The publishers would like to thank the following for their kind
help and advice: *Jonathan Frankel*; *Pippa McCrae*; *Rolls-Royce
plc*; *Charles Schotman*; *Caroline Wise*.

Picture credits
All photographs are from the Earthscape Editions photolibrary
except the following: (c=center t=top b=bottom l=left r=right)

British Alcan Aluminium plc COVER background, 50t, 50c, 50b;
British Petroleum International 4b; *Honda (UK)* 29c; *Rolls-Royce
plc* 21t, 27br; *University of Reading, Rural History Centre* 44t,
47b, 51t; by permission of the *Syndics of Cambridge University
Library* 48 (inset); *Vauxhall Motors Limited* 52b; *ZEFA/
Stockmarket* 18tl.

Contents

(*Left*) Zinc crystals can be seen
clearly on this zinc-plated surface.

(Below) Native gold.

See **Vol. 1: Plastics**, **Vol. 3: Wood and paper**, **Vol. 4: Ceramics**, *and* **Vol. 5: Glass** *for more on these materials.*

(Below) Native gold can be recovered from stream beds by panning. The gold is heavier than the other stones in the river and will stay behind on the pan when all of the sediment has been swirled away.

1: Introduction

Metals are part of our everyday world, and we are familiar with, for instance, iron, silver, gold, copper, and aluminum in the things we use around us. But what do these, and all other metals, have in common, and what sets them apart from other materials?

Every metal is an ELEMENT, that is, a substance that cannot be broken down into a simpler form. Most other materials, for example, CERAMICS and GLASS, are COMPOUNDS of more than one element. Metals are INORGANIC materials, meaning they do not contain carbon. Examples of ORGANIC materials are PLASTICS, wood, and oil.

Every metal can be bent, stretched, is shiny, and conducts electricity and heat well. That makes metals different from, for example, elements such as sulfur or phosphorus, which are very poor conductors of heat or electricity, and which are brittle.

How common are metals?

Metals are very common in the sense that they are a component of most substances. In fact, three-quarters of all of the chemical elements are metals. However, very few metals occur naturally as pure elements. Any that do—such as gold, silver, and copper—are called NATIVE METALS.

Metals that appear in their native form do so because they do not easily combine with other substances. That is, they are chemically relatively unreactive. The fact that gold, for example, always occurs in its native form is what makes it so instantly recognizable.

The majority of metals are, however, very reactive; as a result, they are not found in their native states. Iron and aluminum, for example, appear combined with other elements such as oxygen and sulfur. These compounds make up ROCKS that do not give any hint they contain metal.

When scientists calculate the most abundant metals in the world, they add up the metal content in rocks as well as native metals. On this basis the most common metal is aluminum, followed by iron, calcium, sodium, potassium, and magnesium. Gold is near the bottom of such a list.

When metals are found combined with other substances in rocks, they may add color or some other property to the rock. However, in general, the amount of a metal in a rock is very small. Those rocks that do contain enough metal to make it worth mining for the metal are called metal ores, or just ores.

(Below) Open-pit mining of copper ore in one of the world's biggest mines at Morenci in Arizona. Copper compounds can give a strong green color to ores such as the copper silicate sample shown below, which is called crysocolla $(Cu_2H_2Si_2O_5(OH)_4)$. The mine rock in this picture, however, is mainly brown because iron oxide is the main metal in the ore. Separating the copper from its ore and other ores is a very costly process.

(Left) Hematite (iron ore) contains a large proportion of iron in the form of iron oxide (Fe_2O_3). The reddish-brown color is a sign of the iron.

How metals are made

The properties of a metal are determined by its atomic makeup. When we look at the arrangement of ATOMS in a metal, we find that they are mostly in the form of CRYSTALS. Metals are also usually solid at room temperature.

Pure metals are made of simple crystals. Many are made of sheets of closely packed atoms or electrically charged particles called IONS.

All atoms have two parts: a central area, or nucleus, made of NEUTRONS and PROTONS, and, moving around the nucleus, a number of ELECTRONS. The electrons move in special paths called orbits, known to chemists as shells. Some electrons are found in each shell, and there is a fixed maximum number of electrons that can fit into any shell. In the case of most metals each of the inner shells has a full set of electrons, but the outer shell has only half the electrons that it could possibly hold.

The missing outer electrons make most metals very reactive, and so they readily form compounds with nonmetal elements, such as oxygen. However, metals do not form compounds with one another. That is, a metal such as zinc might form a compound with oxygen, but it would not make a compound with copper. On the other hand, metals will often readily mix with one another, such as when zinc and copper mix to form a material called brass. It is not a compound but a MIXTURE whose parts can be separated again. A mixture of metals is called an ALLOY (see page 23).

Metals can form compounds with nonmetals because nonmetals tend to have more than half the number of electrons they need in their outer shells. A metal and a nonmetal can therefore share electrons, and that is how they form a compound.

(Right) You cannot normally see metal crystals because they are too small. You only notice crystals when they grow under special conditions. For example, barbed wire is often zinc coated (this is called GALVANIZING), but the zinc crystals do not show. The top of the recycling container below is also zinc coated, but during its manufacture the zinc crystals were given the opportunity to grow. They show as a speckled pattern on the lid. Look more closely, and you can see the interlocking crystals very clearly.

This line shows hexagonal packing

"Sea" of electrons

Positive ions of the metal

(Above) In this idealized representation a metal consists of closely packed positive ions embedded in a "sea" of electrons that bond the ions together.

Every ion is surrounded by six others to produce a hexagonal (as above) or cubical packing, and that gives metals their high densities.

The strong bonds between the ions and the free electrons are responsible for the high MELTING POINTS of metals and make them good conductors of heat and electricity.

(Below) The reaction between sodium metal and the nonmetal chlorine produces an ionic crystalline sodium chloride. Rock salt is sodium chloride. Sodium metal can therefore be obtained by breaking the bonds of salt water.

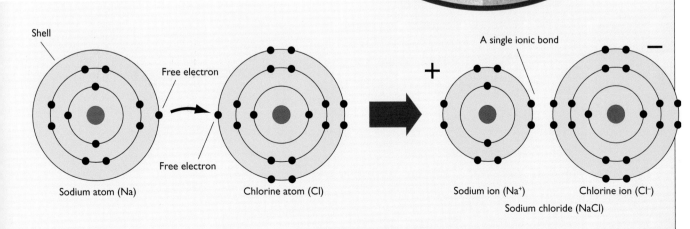

Shell

Free electron

Free electron

A single ionic bond

Sodium atom (Na)

Chlorine atom (Cl)

+

Sodium ion (Na⁺)

−

Chlorine ion (Cl⁻)

Sodium chloride (NaCl)

(Below) The periodic table, showing the large number of metal elements.

KEY
- ■ Metals
- □ Metalloids (semimetals)
- ▨ Nonmetals
- ▨ Inner transition metals

Periods	Groups 1	2	Transition metals										3	4	5	6	7	8 or 0
1	H																	He
2	Li	Be											B	C	N	O	F	Ne
3	Na	Mg											Al	Si	P	S	Cl	Ar
4	K	Ca	Sc	Ti	V	Cr	Mn	Fe	Co	Ni	Cu	Zn	Ga	Ge	As	Se	Br	Kr
5	Rb	Sr	Y	Zr	Nb	Mo	Tc	Ru	Rh	Pd	Ag	Cd	In	Sn	Sb	Te	I	Xe
6	Cs	Ba	Lu	Hf	Ta	W	Re	Os	Ir	Pt	Au	Hg	Tl	Pb	Bi	Po	At	Rn
7	Fr	Ra	Lr	Rf	Db	Sg	Bh	Hs	Mt	Uun	Uuu	Uub		Uuq		Uuh		Uuo

Lanthanide series	La	Ce	Pr	Nd	Pm	Sm	Eu	Gd	Tb	Dy	Ho	Er	Tm	Yb
Actinide series	Ac	Th	Pa	U	Np	Pu	Am	Cm	Bk	Cf	Es	Fm	Md	No

Why metals vary

Because there are so many metals—they make up three-quarters of all known elements—it should not be a surprise to learn that besides having some similar characteristics, metals also vary widely in their properties. Some metals, such as potassium, react violently in air and water, while others, such as tin, remain almost completely unreactive.

Why some metals are hard and others soft

Metals vary widely in their hardness and the ease with which they can be shaped. These properties are also related to the way the atoms are packed together. Metals that are easily bent and squashed probably have some imperfections, which mean that not all atoms are tightly bound to one another. Those metals with fewest imperfections are much more brittle.

(Above) Potassium burns spontaneously in air. In this picture potassium is reacting violently with water to form a solution of potassium hydroxide.

Why metals conduct electricity

Metals conduct electricity because many of the electrons in a metal are not held tightly to their atoms but are free to move around. When a source of electric current is applied to a metal (such as when a wire is connected to both ends of a battery), the electrons are attracted to the positive end of the battery and so make an electric current flow.

For electricity to flow, the electrons inside the metal have to be able to move easily among the atoms. Metals do not all conduct electricity equally well. Copper, silver, gold, and aluminum are among the most conductive, with tungsten being an example of a metal with much lower conductivity.

The conductivity of a metal depends on the pattern of the atoms inside it. The best conductors have a pattern of atoms that is very uniform. Metals with a less uniform pattern of electrons are poorer conductors.

When a metal is warm, the atoms have more energy and vibrate strongly, making it harder for electrons to move between them. When a metal is cooled, the atoms only vibrate slightly, and so the metal conducts electricity far better. At really low temperatures (close to absolute zero, –273°C) metals conduct electricity thousands of times better than at room temperature. This is called SUPERCONDUCTIVITY.

Why some metals are magnetic

When electricity is passed through a metal, it becomes magnetic. In general, the effect is slight, but it is made more noticeable when electricity is passed through a coil of wire. The coil is called an ELECTROMAGNET. Even more curiously, when a block of metal is placed inside the coil of wire, the power of the magnetism is magnified. For most metals the increase is quite modest, just a few percent. But for iron, cobalt, or nickel the magnetism increases by thousands of times.

(Above) This light bulb filament is made from the metal tungsten. It is a relatively poor conductor of heat, and so it slows down the flow of electrons and makes the wire heat up and give out light. Tungsten has a very high melting point; so although it glows white, it does not melt.

(Below) This is a naturally occurring magnetic ore called magnetite. Its magnetism is shown by the iron filings that are attracted to its surface.

Metals that produce a large amount of magnetism when a current passes through them are called ferromagnetic metals. *Ferro* is a word for iron, the most common of these special metals and the one in which the property was first discovered.

Ferromagnetic metals can be taken from the soil and will remain magnetic, although not forever. The softer the material, the faster the magnetism weakens. Most so-called permanent magnets are given a long life by magnetizing a hard metal such as steel (strictly speaking, steel is not a pure metal but has carbon and other elements in it). In this case the loss of magnetism is very slow. That does not mean soft materials have no use. On the contrary, it is often important to have materials that do not keep their magnetism. That is one reason soft iron is used inside electrical transformers.

Whether it is a hard or a soft material, if you heat any metal, the magnetism is gradually lost.

The reactivity of metals

Because metals make up so many of the elements, you can expect some metals to be much more reactive than others.

The least reactive metal is gold. No matter how long you leave it in the air, for example, it will not combine with the oxygen in the air and develop a TARNISH. Instead, it remains bright forever. It is this property that attracted ancient civilizations to it and still attracts us today.

Most metals do react with oxygen, causing the surface to become covered in an oxide coating so thin as to be invisible. Once this coat has formed, most metals will stop reacting. Only the most reactive metals, such as sodium, will continue to react in air.

Metal oxide coatings provide very good protection from reactions at room temperatures in dry air. However, they become less effective at high

(Above) A magnetized piece of iron is a magnet. Its magnetic field is shown here, marked out in iron filings.

(Below) The reactivity series of metals.

Element
Potassium (K)
Sodium (Na)
Calcium (Ca)
Magnesium (Mg)
Aluminum (Al)
Manganese Mn)
Chromium (Cr)
Zinc (Zn)
Iron (Fe)
Cadmium (Cd)
Tin (Sn)
Lead (Pb)
Hydrogen (H_2)
Copper (Cu)
Mercury (Hg)
Silver (Ag)
Platinum (Pt)
Gold (Au)

temperatures. As a result, when metals get hot, they react more readily. Some chemicals, such as water, also have a dramatic effect on the oxide film. This is especially true of iron and steel, whose oxide coat keeps breaking down in the presence of air and water. We see this oxide as RUST.

The presence of a metal speeds up many chemical reactions even though the metal takes no part in the reaction. This is called a CATALYTIC EFFECT. For example, finely divided platinum is used to make the gases coming from car exhausts less polluting. Carbon monoxide and unburned fuel are changed efficiently in the presence of platinum into carbon dioxide and water. That is why the box next to the muffler is called a catalytic converter.

(Above) Silver tarnishes quickly when exposed to air. Air has turned this fork from a shiny gray-white to a dark yellow-black. The upper left corner of the fork has had the tarnish removed using silver polish. The tarnish is caused by reactions with chemicals in the air, principally with hydrogen sulfide gas.

(Below) Lead is a relatively unreactive metal, so it does not corrode. That is why it has traditionally been used to fix glass into window frames.

(Below) An iron chain readily rusts. The zinc-plated chain on the left is not affected.

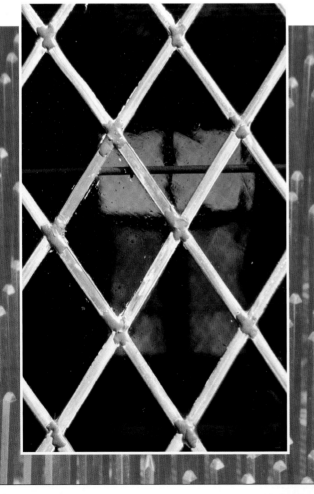

(Below) Although gold is expensive, it is an excellent conductor of electricity and also a relatively unreactive metal. That makes it suitable for specialized applications in electrical circuits.

2: Working with metal

The science of understanding how metals behave, and using this knowledge to make them into things, is called metallurgy.

Why metals are used

Metals are relatively easy to work into different shapes. That, as much as anything, accounts for their widespread use instead of other materials such as fiberglass, plastic, wood, or ceramics.

When a designer chooses a metal for a job, there are two main points considered: the suitability of the metal for the job, and—if there is a choice of metals—which one can be worked most easily. This second point is vital because the faster a thing can be made, the cheaper it is to make. A cheaper metal that is difficult to work can take much longer to make into a product than a slightly costlier metal. Often differences in labor costs far outweigh differences in metal costs.

(Above and opposite) A blacksmith bending an iron bar by first heating it in a furnace *(above)*, then hitting it with a heavy hammer on an anvil. This is an example of a craft level of hotworking.

Metalworking techniques

Metals can be used hot or cold, pure or mixed together (as an alloy). Many processes involve heating, because when metals are heated, they are much easier to work with.

There are seven kinds of metalworking: casting, ROLLING, EXTRUSION, DRAWING, FORGING, SHEET-METAL FORMING, and POWDER FORMING. They can be done either hot or cold.

Hotworking

Metals are made of crystals, usually in the form of tiny particles called grains. This is not easily seen in most metals, although it sometimes shows up in special cases, such as when zinc is plated on steel. The pattern you see is crystals of the metal element zinc (see page 7).

It is important to know about crystals because when a metal is worked with a hammer or a roller, the force involved strains the crystals. Strains can lead to weakness. But if the metal is first heated sufficiently and then worked, the metal will grow a new set of strain-free crystals as it changes shape. That is why many processes are done with hot metal. This is called hotworking. Hotworking does not add strength to the metal.

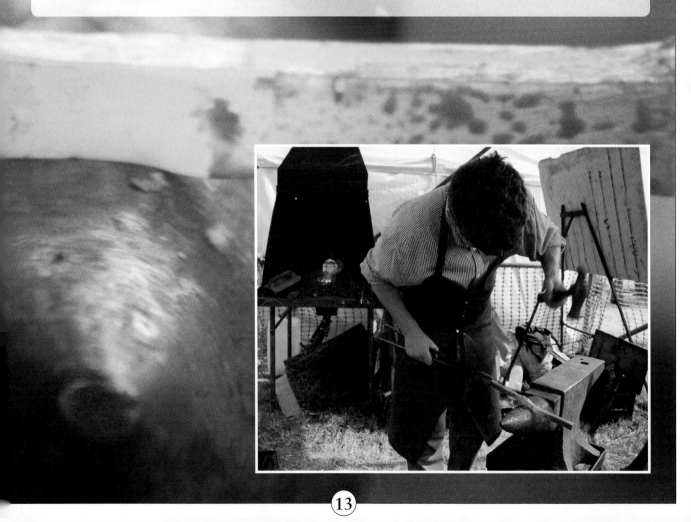

Cold-working

The alternative to hotworking is cold-working. It is done when the metal is too cold for new crystals to grow. Cold-working makes a metal harder and stronger, although it also becomes more brittle and so more liable to crack.

Casting

If the metal is to be made into a large, heavy object, such as the engine block of a car, then it is usually CAST. In this process molten metal is poured into a mold and the metal allowed to set. The mold is then broken open and the casting removed and trimmed to an exact shape.

Casting was well known in the Bronze Age, and most finds from ancient sites are of castings. Castings are still used when a complicated object is needed, for example, door handles and locks.

(Above) All bells are cast. This is the Liberty Bell.

(Below) Fire hydrants are one of the most common objects in the street. They are made by casting.

(Left) The Statue of Liberty is a mixture of casting and cold-working of copper plate.

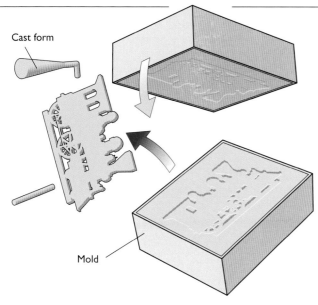

Cast form

Mold

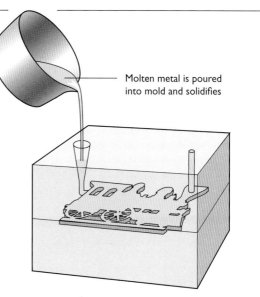

Molten metal is poured into mold and solidifies

(*Above*) To cast something, a mold is first made to the exact shape that the final casting will take. A pattern is needed for this. The pattern is often made from metal or wood. Fine sand or some other appropriate material is then packed around the pattern and the pattern then removed. Alternatively, the pattern can be made from a plastic which will melt and then evaporate as the hot metal flows in. This kind of pattern does not need to be removed before the pouring. In either case a small tube is fitted to allow the metal to be poured into the mold.

When the mold is complete, liquid metal is then poured into the mold. The metal flows into all of the spaces in the mold by gravity.

As the metal flows in, air flows out. Once the mold is full, the metal is allowed to cool. As the metal cools, it shrinks a little. By placing the tube (called a gate) at the top of the casting, more liquid metal can flow in to fill any gaps left by shrinkage. Once the metal is solid, the mold can be broken open and the casting removing.

(*Below*) Casting is a very old technique. This Civil War bronze cannon was cast and then the barrel machined out.

(*Right*) The body of this car water pump is cast.

Bronze castings

Bronze is an ideal material for castings. That is because bronze expands slightly as it solidifies and so pushes against the surface of the mold, thereby reproducing any fine detail. Then, as it cools, it contracts and so pulls away from the mold, making it easy to get out.

For metals such as iron with high melting points the mold is often made of fine silica sand. It will not react chemically with the liquid metal or be distorted by the heat. For metals such as zinc and copper with lower melting points molds can be made from other metals, such as iron.

Casting in sand leaves a rough surface finish, and further work may have to be done to get a smooth surface.

(Below and inset) The brass fitting below (part of a central heating control valve) is cast. The telltale features are slightly rough surfaces (A) and line marking where the halves of the die once met (B).

The steel strand is being continuously cut at the end of its run.

Metal molds produce a much smoother finish. In this case the mold is called a DIE. The die is machined out using LATHES. The metal is often forced into the die under pressure to make sure it fills all of the intricate spaces of the die. This is known as die casting.

Die casts are not cooled in air but quenched in water. That allows the die to be reused quickly. Rapid water cooling also makes the casting stronger, but more brittle, than if it were cooled in air.

To mass produce very small parts, a pattern is made of wax, and then a coating of sand and mud is put on it. More coats are added until the sand and mud make a rigid shell. The wax is then melted out. This method allows a very complex shape to be produced.

Continuous casting is used to mass produce simple objects that will require further work. The metal is poured into one end of the mold; it is cooled by water and then pulled out of the other end. This process is used in the steel industry to make slabs suited to rolling.

(Below) Much molten steel is made into intermediate products by continuous casting processes. Cast steel of this kind needs further processing. Intermediate pieces can be made that are suited to rolling into railroad tracks and beams, bars, wires, and so on. The most common process uses a water-cooled mold, as shown here.

Steel is brought to the casting machine in large containers called ladles.

The steel strand still has a molten core, but it can now be fed continuously along rollers and water jets that cool the steel even further, hold its shape, and keep it from rupturing. The continuously cast strand may be 20 to 40 meters long.

The molten steel is poured through a water-cooled copper mold.
  The shaped steel quickly solidifies on the surface. When this surface "shell" is thick enough, rollers can grab and pull the emerging strand.

(Right) Steel manufacturers also produce cast steel in the form of ingots. They may be as large as 200 tons and are further processed into usable objects.

(Below) Railroad tracks are produced by rolling steel.

(Above) Steel is more easily plastically deformed when it is about 1,200°C. During rolling, the steel is compressed into thinner or narrower pieces usually about an eighth of its original thickness. The large crystals in the usually brittle cast steel are converted into many smaller, longer crystals that make the steel tougher and more DUCTILE.

(Right) By passing a sheet or rod through a series of rollers, the steel can be shaped into a more complex form.

Rolling

The shape of over 90% of metal (including metal that has been through the continuous cast process) is changed by rolling it into a bar or a sheet. This is done in a workshop called a rolling mill. Sheet is the most easily used form of the common metals such as iron, aluminum, and copper.

Rolling is either performed by pushing or pulling the metal through a series of rollers, each making the sheet thinner, or by passing it back and forth through the same rollers whose gap is continually narrowed.

Beams, such as I-beams (or girders) used in buildings and in the track for railroads, are made by rolling the metal while controlling how it can spread out.

Hot rolling is easier but leaves the metal no stronger. Cold rolling is harder but makes the metal stronger, more brittle, and with a smoother finish.

Extruding and drawing

Extruding and drawing is an alternative process to rolling. In this method metals are forced through a die that has been cut to a particular shape. Wire and tubes, as well as complicated shapes, are commonly extruded.

Drawing is the opposite of extruding. Instead of pushing the metal, it is pulled through or into a die. Most wire is drawn. Aluminum beverage cans are also drawn.

(Below) Wire being produced by extrusion through a die.

Die

Wire

Rod

Drawing block

(Below) Large-diameter tubes cannot be produced by drawing. Instead, they are made by rollers, and the seam is then welded and flattened.

(Right) The base and sides of an aluminum beverage can are made by forming a disk of metal. The disk is pushed through a die. The top is added afterward in a rolled seam.

(Left) Handrails made of stainless steel are extruded through dies.

Forging

Forging is a metalworker's term for shaping using a hammer. Remembering that hammering cold metal is one way to strengthen and harden metal, while heating is a way of softening it. Most forging is done with hot metal so that it stays easy to shape.

Most forging is done on very large pieces of metal, the metal being moved around as a hammer repeatedly drops down on an anvil. However, small objects are also forged if an imprint is needed on the surface of the work. All coins are forged cold in large automated presses.

(Left) Some of the finest detail can be produced by cold forging in presses, such as is shown on these coins—the aluminum jiao from China (*above*) and the mixed metal Euro from Europe (*below*).

Pressing

Pressing is a special application of forging. Instead of hammering, sheet metal is usually bent into shape by pressing a sheet of metal over a shaped block. Examples of this are car body panels.

To make the shape change permanent, the pressing has to push the metal beyond the point at which it would bounce back (that is, beyond a value called its elastic limit). This usually involves stretching it by just over 2%.

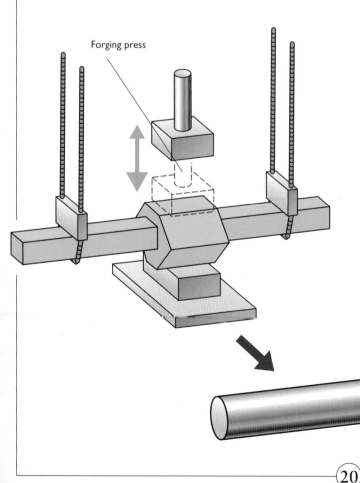

Forging press

Large power plant engine turbine shaft

(*Above*) Gears are powder formed.

(*Below*) Body panels on automobiles and other vehicles, such as the combine harvester and aircraft, are pressed into shape. That is what allows intricate curves to be produced.

Powder forming

None of the processes described so far can produce complex shapes. However, a modern alternative is now available. It is called powder forming. Metals are first reduced to a powder. The powder is then mixed with a liquid and pushed into a die. The powder is next heated, or SINTERED, until the tiny grains of the powder begin to fuse together. This happens below the melting point of the metal.

This process is use routinely with metals, such as platinum and tungsten, that have to be heated to very high temperatures before they will melt. Tungsten filaments for light bulbs are produced this way.

Powder techniques are now also used widely for metals such as iron that do not have high melting points. For example, steel gears are mainly made this way because it saves all of the time and effort that would be needed if the gears had to be cut by machine. Similarly, small parts made of aluminum are also mainly made by pressing powdered aluminum into a die and then heating it.

Most metal powders are produced by spraying the metal as a liquid and allowing the droplets to fall and cool into solid powder.

3: Changing the properties of a metal

All metals change when they are put under a pulling, pushing, or twisting force. If the force is small, the metal will bend a little. When the force is removed, the metal will go back to its original position. This natural springiness is called an ELASTIC CHANGE because the metal goes back to its original shape just as an elastic band would.

When more force is put on a metal, it changes shape permanently. The metal can no longer resist the force, and layers of atoms begin to slide over one another. This is called a PLASTIC CHANGE (not to be confused with plastic as a material). When the material is changed in this way and the force removed, it will still have elastic properties as long as the force is small. For example, a paper clip has to be formed by applying enough force to bend the wire into shape. But when the wire has been shaped, it is springy (elastic) enough to be used as a clip.

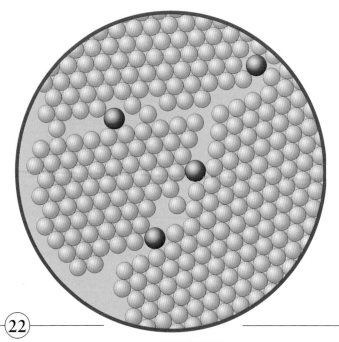

(Above and below) Alloying disrupts the crystals' slipping planes, effectively locking one part of a crystal against another. The locking atoms are those of the alloying metal. You can see that not many atoms are needed, and so alloys with just a few percent of another metal may produce considerable changes in character as compared to the pure metal.

Heating and beating

Some metals can be made stronger simply by repeatedly heating them in a fire and then beating them with a hammer. This is commonly done to iron and titanium. It was traditionally the way that a blacksmith both shaped and hardened his wares (see pages 12 and 13).

In some cases the metal needs to have properties on the surface that are different from those inside. One example of this is when the surface of iron or steel has to be hardened, for instance, to make a knife. Heating iron or steel in a fire and then beating it mixes some carbon atoms (from the fuel) into the surface. A final heating without beating allows some of the softness to return. This is the process called TEMPERING.

Another way to harden a metal is to work it while it is cold, for example, by passing it under a hammer (a process called forging) or through rollers (called rolling). These actions break up the layers of atoms and so prevent them from easily moving past one another.

Alloying

An alternative to physically moving the atoms into new patterns is to use mixtures of several metals. Most metals mix easily when they have been melted. A mixture of metals is called an alloy. The metal that makes up the majority of an alloy is called a BASE METAL. The most common base metals are iron, aluminum, and copper.

When an alloying metal is added, the atoms of the alloying metal fit in among the atoms of the base metal and keep layers of the base metal from slipping past one another as easily. That is why the alloy is harder than the base metal.

Alloys are made by melting each of the metals and then mixing them in the proportions needed. Because metals oxidize much more easily when they are hot, care has to

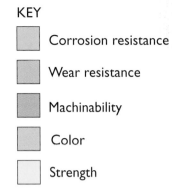

KEY

Corrosion resistance

Wear resistance

Machinability

Color

Strength

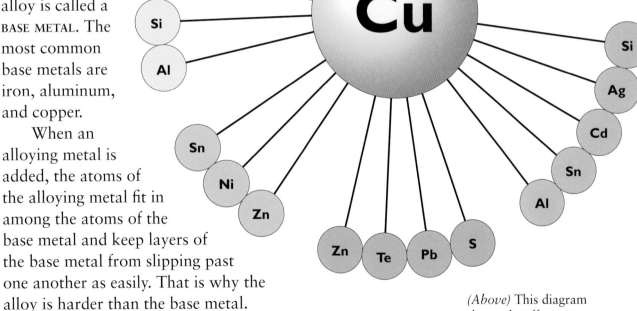

(Above) This diagram shows the effects on copper of alloying it with other metals.

be taken to keep oxygen away from the molten alloy. This has traditionally been done by allowing a SLAG of waste to float on the surface, although modern processes often do away with slag and mix the metals in a vacuum.

A base metal can be made stronger by alloying it with other metals. Indeed, the vast majority of metals used today are alloys of a number of metals. Stainless steel is a common example of a metal alloy

(*Above*) Brass is one of the most widely used alloys. Brass is usually made from 64% copper and 36% zinc. The more zinc, the harder the alloy. Brass is often used for corrosion-resistant decorative purposes such as door hardware. It is much harder and stronger than copper and zinc, and it machines well.

The most common mixture of brass contains 36% zinc and is known as common brass. The properties of brass can be altered significantly by adding small quantities of other elements. Those most commonly used are lead, tin, aluminum, manganese, iron, nickel, arsenic, and silicon. For example, by adding up to 3% lead, the machinability of brass can be improved significantly.

Copper-rich brasses have special uses, such as making the percussion caps of ammunition. Those

with between 10 and 20% zinc are called gilding metals and are used for decorative brasswork and jewelry. This form of brass takes an enamel well and is easy to glaze.

As the amount of zinc is increased even further, the brass develops the property of being easily shaped when hot. This material is used to make inexpensive but complex engineering shapes that are easy to machine.

However, even higher amounts of zinc make the alloy more likely to corrode when the brass is put in water. To counteract this problem, arsenic is added to the alloy.

Tin can also be added to brass to improve its corrosion resistance. Tin-zinc-copper brasses in which there is 1% tin are known as admiralty brass because of their suitability for use on ships.

(*Left and below*) Bronze is typically made from 78% copper and 12% tin. The less tin, the softer the metal alloy. Usually no more than 25% is added. Adding tin makes a copper alloy that is more corrosion resistant. Adding zinc and lead to the bronze alloy makes the metal more suitable for casting.

An alloy with about nine-tenths copper and equal proportions of the other metals is called gunmetal and was commonly used in cannons. It is corrosion resistant and has good machinability.

Copper

Tin

whose base metal is iron and whose alloying metals include chromium, magnesium, and molybdenum. The world's first really useful alloy was bronze, an alloy of copper and tin.

Alloys often have properties very different from the metals they contain. Quite often an alloy has a melting point lower than the melting point of the metals from which it is made. Solder is a good example of this (62% tin and 38% lead).

Alloying will usually help make the base metal more resistant to corrosion and sometimes even reduce the cost of using the metal by making it more workable.

In some cases it is useful for an alloy to look like an expensive pure metal although it can be made more cheaply. Gold and silver are commonly alloyed for this purpose (although alloying also improves their qualities, especially by making gold harder and so less liable to wear away).

Sterling silver is the name for the silver alloy used in jewelry. In this case 7.5% of copper is used.

(*Below*) Solder, an alloy of lead and tin, has a lower melting point than either of them. It is used to seal joints that remain electrically conductive. Solder is used in virtually all printed circuits.

Modern coins that look like silver are actually an alloy of 75% copper and 25% nickel.

A piece of jewelry made of pure gold is called 24-carat gold. Most jewelry is, however, an alloy. For example, the commonly used 18-carat gold is only 75% gold.

In industry many alloys are based on aluminum. Aluminum-magnesium-silicon alloys become stronger when they are heated because heating precipitates fine particles that lock the alloy together. They are also valued for their corrosion resistance. They are used, for example, in storm doors, window frames, truck cabs and trailers, boats, and "alloy" wheels of cars.

Aluminum-copper alloys are extremely strong but are not as corrosion resistant. They are used in aircraft wings but have to be coated with aluminum to add corrosion resistance.

(*Above*) Fuses are alloys designed to have a low melting point.

(*Right*) Nickels, dimes, and quarters are all alloys designed to look like silver.

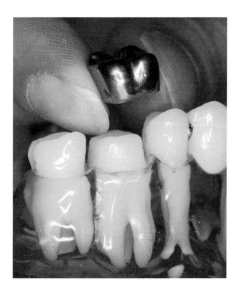

(*Above*) This gold crown is not pure gold. It would be too soft. Rather, it is an alloy containing 60% gold, 22% silver, 12% copper, 4% palladium, and 1% zinc.

Porcelain crowns are supported by a silvery-white metal containing 57% palladium, 30% silver, 6% tin, and 2% zinc. These proportions achieve the best combination of no corrosion and strength in the porcelain.

(*Below*) This is sterling silver, an alloy with copper.

(*Below*) This gold ring is actually an alloy and not pure gold. Pure gold is soft and wears away easily.

More expensive but more lightweight are aluminum-copper-lithium alloys. Their main use is for aircraft manufacture because reducing weight is of prime concern.

The highest strength alloys are aluminum-zinc-magnesium. Some also contain copper. They can be treated to reduce the likelihood of METAL FATIGUE. Aluminum-silicon alloys are used for welding wire because the silicon makes the molten aluminum more runny.

Another example is when the surface needs to be protected from corrosion. Anodizing is a treatment applied to aluminum to make it harder and more corrosion resistant (see page 32).

(Left) "Steel" hawsers used, for example, on suspension bridges; they are usually an alloy. If they were not, they would rust.

(Below) Stainless steel is an alloy. It is used to superb effect in the Gateway Arch, St. Louis.

(Below) Virtually every piece of metal on this fighter plane is an alloy; in particular, most of the fuselage is made of aluminum alloys. By making alloys, metals can be given exactly the right qualities for their purpose.

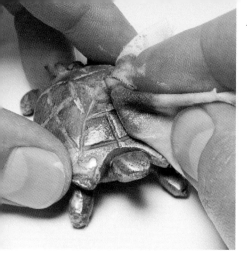

Making metal resist corrosion

CORROSION is a surface chemical reaction that takes place between a metal and its environment—usually a combination of air and water. Some reactive liquids, such as acids and strong alkalis like potassium hydroxide, can also cause severe corrosion.

When a metal corrodes in water, for example, by being left out in the rain, the metal reacts chemically with water in the presence of air, and the metal atoms lose some electrons to the water. In time holes form in the corroding part, and it become useless or dangerous.

Of the common metals only gold does not react with air or water at all. Others, like chromium, react very poorly and so are almost corrosion free. Copper is typical of metals that react in such a way as to protect themselves. Copper develops a protective green coat. Thus a newly roofed building using copper may start out as an orangy color, but it soon changes to green. This is called a PATINA. Once formed, the coating is stable.

(Above) Copper and alloys that contain a high proportion of copper develop a greenish patina of copper carbonate when exposed to the atmosphere (see also the Statue of Liberty on page 14). The patina protects the metal below it. But if it is regarded as unsightly, it can be removed temporarily using cleaning agents.

(Left) Paint has traditionally been used to protect steel. Once it wears away, however, the steel quickly rusts.

(Above) Aluminum is self-protecting, which is one reason it can be used for food containers.

Unfortunately, the most commonly used metal—mild steel—does not develop a stable oxide coat. The corroded coating on mild steel is called RUST.

Paints and lacquers

Vulnerable metals can be protected by covering them with a nonreacting material, for example, paint. Paint, lacquer, or some other similar unreactive surface material is fine if the surface is not subjected to high temperatures or hard wear. Paints are also unsuitable for surfaces used to prepare, store, or cook foods because flakes of paint could get into the food.

(Left, right, and below) Rust used to be the death of cars because the steel from which they were made was insufficiently protected from corrosion. Many layers of surface coating now help ensure that rust now only affects cars after many years. That is why cars now come with six or more years of bodywork rust warranty.

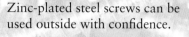

Zinc-plated steel screws can be used outside with confidence.

(Above) Zinc would react with the acidic contents of many cans. So, tin plating is used as skin to protect the iron that goes into making up most of a "tin" can. However, if you scratch the surface tin plating on a tin can, the iron below will soon rust if exposed to air and moisture.

(Below) A common decorative protective coating is chromium. Here it is plated over a bathroom faucet.

Plating

Another, more durable way to protect things is to plate the surface of the metal with another metal that does not corrode. That is the purpose of tin plating on steel cans. Zinc is also plated onto steel to make galvanized steel, for example, in barbed wire.

Nickel and chromium are other noncorroding (almost inert) metals that are plated over other metals. They also have the advantage of producing an attractive, shiny silvery surface.

Faucets and many other household items are chromium plated. Chromium does not stick easily to steel, so a plating of copper and nickel has first to be applied to the steel, and then the chromium is plated onto the copper. All plating is done using a bath of liquid through which an electric current passes.

Galvanic protection

The term "galvanic protection" comes from Luigi Galvani, a famous Italian scientist who investigated electricity in the 18th century. Zinc is often plated on to steel, and in this form it is called galvanized steel. If a chip is made in the zinc exposing the iron, the zinc, the iron, and the water act as a battery. The zinc will lose electrons even more readily than iron, and so the zinc corrodes, leaving the iron untouched.

Cadmium and aluminum are other metals used for galvanic and oxide protection. The steel of exhaust systems is commonly aluminum plated.

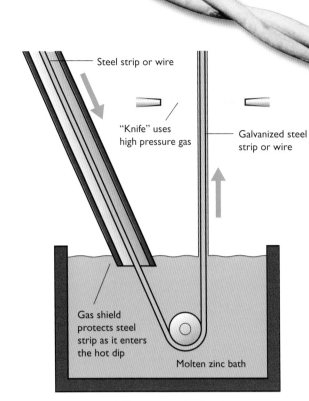

Steel strip or wire

"Knife" uses
high pressure gas

Galvanized steel
strip or wire

Gas shield
protects steel
strip as it enters
the hot dip

Molten zinc bath

Two different methods of
protecting a sheet of metal using
zinc, a process called galvanizing:
by hot dipping in zinc (*above*)
and by electroplating (*below*).

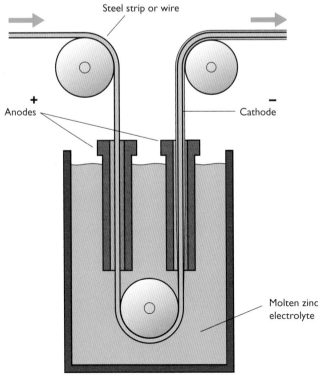

Steel strip or wire

+
Anodes

−
Cathode

Molten zinc
electrolyte

(Left) Galvanized
barbed wire has a
surface coating of zinc.

(Above) Zinc-plated
steel—often called
corrugated iron—
has long been an
inexpensive building
material.

(Above) Much
modern cutlery
is stainless steel.

(*Left*) Anodized duralumin alloy dog collar—used almost entirely for its decorative effect and light weight.

Galvanic protection is also used to guard the hulls of ships, which are constantly bathed in seawater. To protect a hull, large blocks of magnesium are attached to the hull. The blocks, the seawater, and the hull act as a "battery," protecting the steel hull by sacrificing the magnesium blocks rather than the hull. From time to time the blocks have to be replaced because they quickly become corroded.

Anodizing

Some metals protect themselves by naturally forming a thin oxide coat when exposed to air. Oxides do not react with water, and so they form a natural barrier to more corrosion. The layer of oxide is often so thin it is invisible. Stainless steel and aluminum protect themselves with oxide films of this kind. Aluminum is also often given added protection (and sometimes color) by ANODIZING.

During anodizing the object to be treated is dipped in a bath of electrically conducting liquid. It is usually dilute sulfuric acid. The object is connected to an electricity supply in such a way as to make it the positive connection, or anode, in a circuit. As the electricity flows, it causes a layer of oxide to be deposited, or plated, on the object being anodized. By putting a dye in the acid, the plating can be colored and the objects made more decorative.

(*Left*) Anodized duralumin alloy climbing clips (carabiners).

Enameling

A layer of glass or RESIN (plastic) can also protect metal. It is used on some household metal goods and (whether glass or resin) is called ENAMEL. Enamel is commonly applied to kitchen appliances such as stoves and dishwashers. The enamel layer does not react with water (it is inert), and at the same time, it sticks hard to the steel and has an attractive appearance. Baths made of steel are also enameled. Because most enamel is a poor conductor of heat, the bases of enameled pots and pans are not enameled. Glass-enameled surfaces are brittle and liable to chip, resin ones far less so.

(Below) Enamel paint can often be distinguished by its slightly rippled effect when seen in reflective light.

(Below) The blue cooking pots in the foreground of this market scene are old-fashioned enameled pots with a glass surface coating on metal. The surface is hard but brittle, as shown by this detail *(left)*.

Alloying for corrosion resistance

Sometimes the metal itself needs to be made corrosion resistant, rather than coating it with a protective surface. That is achieved by alloying, as mentioned earlier in the chapter. However, alloying considerably alters the properties of a material as well as adding to the cost, and so the alloy route may not be desirable. That is why, for example, most car body panels are still made of coated steel rather than of stainless steel.

(Below) A range of alloys in a door lock. The external alloys are chosen for their corrosion resistance and attractive appearance, the internal alloys for their strength and resistance to cutting.

Inside the lock the surface finish is not as important for decorative effect. This type of steel resists rusting and is tough but is cheaper and is unfinished.

A carbon-steel deadbolt must stand up to being forced by an intruder. This kind of steel is difficult to cut.

Chromium-plated knob for highly reflective decorative effect. On the inside of the door it does not have to stand up to the same effects of weathering as the outside.

Stainless-steel cover. This steel is needed to stand up to the harsh weather that affects the outside of the lock.

Strip of spring steel is part of the locking mechanism.

Chromium-plated brass key. The brass is easy to cut into shape. The chromium produces the decorative effect of making it a similar color to the steel. The key does not have to be especially tough. However, the brass will fracture if the key gets stuck and too much turning force is used.

(Above and below) Cold bending metal will make a metal exceed its elastic limit and experience plastic change. Repeated bending of this kind may lead to metal fatigue.

Preventing metal fatigue

One serious problem that can develop in metals is metal fatigue. It happens when a piece of metal is squashed, pulled, or twisted many times. A crack and then a break occur after some time even though the force on the metal might be much lower than the force normally needed to break it.

Metal fatigue has been known for over a century, but it has become more of a problem with modern equipment. The first spectacular crash of a Comet aircraft in 1954 led to widespread concern about metal fatigue.

It has not been easy to understand what causes metal fatigue, although certain metal alloys have been found that are much less prone to this failure. These alloys are used in modern aircraft, in replacement body parts, and elsewhere. Another way of reducing the chances of fatigue is to make sure that designs do not cause the buildup of a force in a small area, for example, where an engine is attached to an aircraft wing.

4: Metals through the ages

Metals are used so widely today that you may not realize that for much of prehistory people hardly used metals at all. Metals were much harder to work than wood and could not be obtained in such large amounts as stone.

The first metals to be used were native metals such as gold and copper. But these metals are soft and have limited uses. All other metals had to be extracted from rock, and this proved a challenge that could not be overcome for thousands of years.

For these reasons metals were first used sparingly and largely for their decorative effects. The attractive appearance of gold and silver made them desirable as jewelry, but copper also found a use as shields and swords. As other metals were discovered, a wider and wider range of applications were found for them, new metals often replacing the ones used previously for the same task. In this chapter we describe just a few of the vast number of uses to which metals have been put through history and the way that changes in metal technology affected them.

Early metalworking

Mankind's use of metal stretches back nearly 7,000 years. The first metals to be used were native gold, silver, and copper, in part because they were easy to work and also because they were easy to recognize in the ground. Gold was probably first noticed as nuggets in riverbeds. Silver occurs more often as veins. Copper can occur as large pieces among rocks.

(Above) Gold was used earlier than any other known metal.

Because these metals are soft, they are easily worked by hammering with stone tools. They will also melt, or at least soften, at the low temperatures of open fires.

Gold is the easiest of the native metals to work because a large sheet can be formed simply by hammering together small nuggets. The gold does not need to be heated or treated in any way. Gold is also attractive. As a result, one of its first uses was for jewelry (although it was also made into armor breastplates as protection in battle).

(Above) The first exploitation of metal probably came about as a result of accidentally using an ore as a hearth rock in cooking. Part of the rock got soft so that it could be worked, or it may have dripped from the rock as pure metal.

To get small pieces of other native metals such as copper or silver to mix together, they must be heated until they melt. The accidental discovery of how solid metals turn into liquids and run together was probably made in an open hearth used for cooking. If the rocks used for the hearth were rich in copper or silver, the metals could easily have been seen as they flowed out.

The Bronze Age

Although the earliest known examples of melting copper to make axe heads can be dated back 6,000 years, the time in history when metal became an important material was the Bronze Age.

The Bronze Age began in different places at different times. In Asia and Europe it began between 5,000 and 4,000 years ago. It was perhaps as accidental in its beginnings as the finding and working of gold.

Bronze is a mixture (alloy) of copper and tin. Some rocks naturally contain both metals. Stannite, for example, is an ORE that contains a mixture of copper, iron, and tin, and so the substance that was produced when it was heated was bronze.

Bronze was probably first discovered in the Middle East. Bronze is harder than copper or tin. It also has a lower melting point than tin and is easily poured

(Above) Native copper.

into molds to make shapes such as bowls (it is easy to cast). It also stands up well to the weather (it is slow to CORRODE).

Knowledge of bronze spread gradually to western Asia and then to Europe as traders took finished bronze to trade for other goods.

Once the properties of bronze had been discovered, people then sought rocks with copper and tin in them. The tin ore cassiterite is, for example, quite easy to recognize from other pebbles in a river because the pebbles are very heavy for their size.

The Iron Age

There was a long gap in history between the use of soft metals and the later development of harder metals such as iron. Most metals occur in rocks combined with oxygen. They are called OXIDES. Others combine with sulfur to form SULFIDES. As compounds, the metals often have a dull color and do not look much like the pure element. When they were heated, metals did not flow from these rocks.

However, the early fires contained burned wood—charcoal. Charcoal is mostly carbon. The carbon combined with the oxygen in the rock, and it is this chemical reaction that released the metal and allowed it to run free. We now call this process SMELTING, and it is still the basis for releasing metals from rocks.

(*Above*) Roman times began in the Bronze Age, and the empire collapsed in the Iron Age. This is a bronze Roman coin showing the Emperor Hadrian. It was minted some time between A.D. 126 and 138. Despite having been buried in soil since that time, the coin still shows a lot of detail from the original striking. This demonstrates the resistance of bronze to corrosion.

Metals for coins

A coin is a small piece of metal with marks on its surface that tell its value. Coins have little competition from other materials. Metal coins are easily exchangeable, are small and easy to carry, and do not readily wear out (lose their markings) or break.

Historically, people bartered with precious metals and often made them into both jewelry and coinage. The Vikings, for example, wore armband decorations of silver and simply cut pieces off (called hack silver) to pay their bills.

The first metal coins were issued in the 7th century B.C. The process for making coins was to cast blank disks using molds into which the metal was poured. The disks were allowed to become solid, and then they were reheated to make them soft. The marks on the surface were then hammered onto them using a die made of a much harder metal, such as bronze or iron. In many cases iron dies could be hard punched onto the blank.

The kind of metal used depended on what was thought of as precious. Gold and silver were common, but other metals such as iron also went into coins. Because people were used to getting something of value in exchange for their goods, the size and weight of the coins were often equal to their value as raw metal. However, as the value of these metals rose and fell, the value of the coins also rose and fell. That caused all kinds of trading problems.

To mark the fact that they were official coins, beginning with Alexander the Great, one side was stamped with images of the ruler's head, gods, or heroes.

None of these early coins were of uniform weight or size. By the 15th century machines could be made that gave all coins the same size and weight, and so modern coins developed. The metal content of coins has also changed, although coins still containing precious metals have survived (mainly as special gifts) right up to the present day (for example, golden eagles, golden sovereigns, rands).

Ancient minting was done by placing a blank on a die, putting another die on top of it, and then hammering the top die. That left an imprint on both surfaces. It also distorted the shape of the blank, so that many early coins have an irregular form. A die lasted for perhaps 10,000 to 20,000 coins, after which new dies had to be made.

By the Middle Ages the dies lasted much longer because they were made out of steel. The steel was then hardened by putting the die in a bed of charcoal in a sealed box, which was then put into a furnace. As the die got hot, more carbon was soaked up by the steel, making it harder.

At this time there was widespread forgery of coins—they were being made to look like a precious metal although they were made of alloys of cheaper metals. For example, a copper coin could be silver plated to make it look like a silver coin. Because many coins were still made of precious metal, there also had to be a safeguard against someone filing the edge of the coins and melting down the filings. As a result, a serrated edge was put on the coins. Counterfeiting has remained a problem. However, since coins are used now only for low values, it is less bothersome.

Today blanks are no longer cast. Instead, coins are punched out of sheets of metal. Modern minting is very highly automated, with around 2,000 coins being produced by each machine each minute.

The most important issue of new coins in recent times was the production of hundreds of millions of Euro coins at the beginning of 2002, when many European countries began to use the same currency.

(Below) A Roman legionary soldier. His helmet was made from copper in early legions. But as iron became available, it was made from iron. The javelin tip is iron, the body armor is also iron, as is the sword (*gladius*) hanging from the belt. On the shield only the boss is iron; the rest is wood.

In practice metals still do not normally run free from rocks unless another substance is present. This material is called a FLUX. Iron oxide is a flux, and it is commonly found in rocks. As a result, by chance all of the materials needed to release metals from their rocks were present in some ancient hearths.

Iron melts at a much higher temperature (1,540°C) than copper, gold, silver, lead, or tin. As a result, iron would not have been separated from its rock in simple charcoal fires. But since iron occurred naturally in many of the rocks used to obtain copper, occasionally the temperature in the hearth rose enough for the iron to change from a solid to a spongy metal paste, something we now call a BLOOM. It contained impurities that we now call slag. The first use of iron therefore dates from the Bronze Age, just as the first use of bronze dates from the Stone Age.

By 1200 B.C., however, iron was being more widely used. This is the date usually considered to be when the Bronze Age gave way to the Iron Age. Again, not all regions changed at the same time, so the Iron Age started in some regions much earlier than others.

In the Middle East metalworkers realized that a higher-temperature fire could be made by using bellows. They also realized that these temperatures could be reached more easily in a special kind of oven rather than on an open hearth.

By making these two changes, fires could be made to reach temperatures of about 1,200°C. However, the iron they made was not fully molten, but a plastic mixture of iron and slag. The iron was made more usable by reheating and hammering it many times. During this process the slag was mostly removed. The finished material—the result of hammering—is WROUGHT IRON.

Iron comes in two forms: wrought iron and cast iron. Cast iron was discovered much later than wrought iron. To make cast iron, the iron has to be fully molten. Then it soaks up much more carbon from the fuel. Cast iron with about 4% carbon is brittle, and it cannot be forged like wrought iron. But it can be poured into a mold and made into complicated shapes.

Pure wrought iron is soft and was not directly usable for weapons. But as better furnaces were made, higher temperatures were reached. In the hotter furnaces more carbon from the charcoal was soaked up by the iron. When even tiny amounts of carbon are added to iron, it becomes much harder. It becomes steel.

The first steel was made in Egypt, but the centers of production quickly moved to India and across the Middle East.

Steel was made in two stages: After the iron had been hammered to remove the slag, it was wrapped up in wood chips and put in a sealed clay container. The carbon in the chips was soaked up (absorbed) by the surface of the iron, making steel. Reheating and forging (hammering) the steel produced metal that would make fine weapons such as daggers and swords that could hold a sharp edge. The Middle East, and especially the blacksmiths of Damascus in Syria, were renowned for their weapons, and this kind of steel became known as Damascus steel.

Blacksmiths then discovered that by dipping hot steel in cold water (a process called QUENCHING), the steel could be made even harder. Unfortunately, this also makes the steel more brittle. However, by reheating it to between 250 and 500°C and then cooling it in air (a process called tempering), the steel could be made tough as well as hard, with lessened brittleness and fewer internal stresses. This could be done by the middle Iron Age (about 1,000 B.C.).

Other metals used in ancient times

Iron has been the most important metal for most of history. However, some other metals also had important parts to play. Brass (an alloy of zinc and copper) was discovered about 30 B.C. It was quickly adopted and was, for example, used for coins during the Roman Empire.

(Above) Metal was a very precious and expensive commodity. For this reason it was used with care. That is why it is found coiled up and also in places where there was wealth. This medieval wooden door is faced with sheet iron—a very expensive thing to do at the time.

Swords and daggers

Swords and daggers have been the most important tools for hand-to-hand fighting throughout history. Despite the handgun, knives continue to be an important piece of weaponry.

Swords were often the most treasured possession of a fighting man, and many swords were buried with their owner. In Viking times swords were often "killed" by bending them when their owner died and so making them unusable.

The sword is made of three parts: the blade, the guard, and the hilt. Throughout much of history the blade was wide and designed for slashing. First made of copper and bronze, the blades of swords and daggers gradually became made of iron or steel. The finest swords were made of strips of steel beaten out into a blade after being heated in a charcoal fire.

A very effective form of a slashing and cutting blade is the curved blade, called the scimitar by the Turks. A modified form of it was used by the cavalry in Europe and North America where it was known as a saber.

Armor

Armor is a key resource for any fighting force. Wars have been won and lost entirely due to superior or inferior armor. Metal armor has always been expensive, and in ancient times only very wealthy peoples could afford it.

The Greeks and Romans used armor in the form of small plates. The alternative was armor made of small loops, called chain mail.

The Romans were one of the first peoples to give their fighting soldiers (and not just their generals) body armor. But soon chain mail became available to the peoples beyond the empire.

The earliest body armor protected the head (in the form of a helmet) and the body in the form of breastplates and back plates. However, after Roman times the metal plates were dropped in favor of coats made of chain mail.

They were all designed to protect the wearer from the slashing effect of a sword (swords were not designed to skewer but to slice). Nobles then sought extra protection in the form of a shield.

Full armor plating developed after chain mail, probably by about 1200. At first it was used on top of the chain mail to protect areas such as elbows and knees. In time the plated armor became sufficiently strong that it could be used instead of chain mail everywhere except under the arms and between the legs. As a result of better protection, the shield did not need to be so large, and so it became smaller and easier to use.

The invention of bullets and the use of gunpowder in the 16th and 17th centuries made armor instantly obsolete since bullets could easily go through the thin metal sheet or chain mail.

This was, however, not the end of armor plate. With advances in understanding of metals, special hard mixtures, or alloys, of metals were developed that could even stop modern bullets.

The first widely used modern armor was known as a flak jacket and worn in World War I. It was designed to protect against fragments of exploding shells rather than bullets. It used special alloy steel plates stitched into a fabric vest

Bullets are made of lead (although armor-piercing bullets are made with steel tips). Body armor made of metal has to be strong enough to stop the lead bullet. Body armor made from many layers of nylon or Kevlar® works by causing the soft lead of the bullet to flatten, turning mushroom-shaped. As soon as it is flattened, the energy of the bullet can be spread out among the fibers of the many layers of the vest.

The increase in terrorism in modern times has led to widespread use of body armor by police and security forces, but none of it is made with metal. Metal armor plating continues to be used for vehicles, ships, and planes.

(Below) Modern metal armor is restricted to vehicles, ships, and planes.

See **Vol. 1: Plastics** and **Vol. 7: Fibers** for more on kevlar.

Breastplate

Gauntlet

(*Above*) Body armor in the Middle Ages was made from sheet iron and chain mail. The parts were riveted together to allow a small amount of movement.

Lead was another metal discovered in ancient times. It was originally found in rocks containing silver. The Greeks were the first to use lead, although it is perhaps best known for its use in water systems by the Romans. Their word for lead was *plumbum*, and they used it to make water pipes, hence our modern word "plumbing" for water-pipe work.

Mercury was another metal that was known in ancient times. This metal also has the distinction of being a liquid at room temperature. Mercury has many uses, but it also has the disadvantage of being extremely poisonous.

Metals before the Industrial Revolution

Ancient civilizations recognized that metals could sometimes do what other materials could not. Weaponry was one of the first examples. The reason for this is that we have always lived in troubled times, and so the first task is to protect yourself. Only then can you have the time and luxury to use metals for the other things you might want (see page 43).

We would not think the metals used for swords in ancient times—bronze and copper—very suitable because they were soft, could not keep a sharp edge, and were easily damaged in battle. Copper blades were made somewhat harder by hammering them. Nevertheless, they were, in their day, state of the art. As new metals—iron and steel—became available, they were first put to use in making better weapons.

However, metals can be used to such an extent that they become a liability rather than a help. In the Middle Ages in Europe body armor was developed so far that a man could be totally enclosed in a suit of iron armor. But it weighed so much, he could not move around. He could only do battle on a horse, but the weight meant that only a big horse was built strong enough to carry him.

Knights were hoisted onto their horses using cranes. Once the knight was upright, all he could do was to charge around with a lance. The use of a sword was very difficult because of the risk of toppling off the horse. With his visor down he could not hear anyone or be heard.

These suits of armor were so unwieldy that it was easy for a group of lightly armed men on foot to overwhelm a knight in all his armor. As a result, this extensive use of metal for body armor was abandoned.

The use of metals changed dramatically when explosives appeared. Cannon and rifles required metals that were much sturdier than those used in hand-to-hand fighting. Cannon, for example, had to be massively built because, at first, the technology was not available to make strong steels.

The earliest guns were cast from brass or bronze in the same foundries as bells. These cannon were expensive and did not stand up well to explosives. It was only when wrought iron became available in the 14th century that cannon became widespread. The muzzle of the cannon was made from long slats of iron that had to be beaten together to make a tube. This tube had to be reinforced with a number of hoops just like a barrel. Cannonballs were made

(Above) Plows were first made of wood, but the plowing tip wore down quickly. At the same time, metal was expensive and difficult to work two millennia ago, and so the only metal part on this plow is a sheath to cover the plowing tip.

(Below) Casting bells was a metalworking skill that developed in the European Middle Ages.

(Right) Cannon were made first in bronze and then iron and then bronze again.

of cast iron. Then it was discovered how to improve the bronze and make it stand up better to explosions, so cast bronze cannons came back into fashion.

Small arms, such as muskets, rifles, and pistols, were developed in the 15th century. At first they were built like miniature cannons, but the development of better steels allowed them to follow a separate history. They were needed in wars by the millions. People also realized that making them out of identical parts would allow the guns to be repaired easily. As a result, the construction of rifles and pistols was standardized. This was the forerunner of the mass production system.

Bullets and shells

A bullet is a small projectile that is fired from a pistol, machine gun, or rifle. Larger-size (caliber) projectiles are called shells.

The first bullets were made by dropping molten lead down a tall tower. As it fell, it split up into tiny balls, reaching the ground as solid shot.

As a result of the way they were made, the first bullets were round. These bullets could not, however, be fired very accurately. To improve the accuracy, narrow corkscrew-shaped cuts were made in the inside of the gun barrel. This effect, called rifling, made the bullet spin as it moved and so travel in a straighter line. A projectile-shaped bullet works much better in these circumstances, and so round bullets were replaced by the modern ones from about 1825.

Most pistol bullets are made of a mixture of lead and antimony alloy enclosed in a case of copper or copper-plated steel. Rifle and machine gun bullets are made with steel cases.

Armor-piercing bullets have the lead replaced with hardened steel.

The lead inside the bullet gives the bullet momentum and so makes it move through the air without being significantly slowed by air resistance. The casing, or jacket of copper or steel, ensures the soft lead interior does not splay out as it enters the target. If the casing is left off the front of the bullet, the lead deforms when it hits the target and makes a much bigger wound. This kind of "expanding bullet" is outlawed by all nations for war.

Although the main use for metals was for military purposes, other people had pressing needs for metal as well. There were some things that people wanted to do that simply could not be done with other materials. Most important of them was the development of machinery. People used iron on the tips of wooden plowshares, although they rarely used expensive metal for an entire tool.

The Industrial Revolution

Over the centuries people gradually improved their ways of extracting metals from rocks and turning them into useful things. Iron was by far the most important. However, it was still made using charcoal from trees; and in some parts of the world, England in particular, so much charcoal was needed that the supply of trees was running out! This led people to seek another way of making iron.

(*Above, left, and below*) The Bessemer converter from iron to steel. It was one of the cornerstone developments of the Industrial Revolution.

The need to find a different fuel eventually led to the success of Abraham Darby in England, who in 1709 discovered how to use COKE in a furnace instead of charcoal. Because coke was made from coal, and coal was available in huge amounts, the price of fuel for making iron fell dramatically. This led to a huge increase in the amount of iron made. By 1740 a reliable way of making steel in a special heat-resistant bowl called a CRUCIBLE had been found. These changes were a vital part of the time that came to be known as the INDUSTRIAL REVOLUTION.

During the 19th century the main changes were in making iron and steel on a large scale. The blast furnace was invented by Henry Bessemer in 1855. The large-scale production of steel—using the open hearth furnace—was also developed at this time by William and Friedrich Siemens in Britain and by Pierre and Émile Martin in France.

(Above) Abraham Darby constructed the world's first iron bridge between 1777 and 1779 in Shropshire, England. The nearby town called itself Ironbridge. Since people were unused to working in large sizes of metal, the structure was actually based on the design the bridge would have had if it had been made of wood. The bridge is still used as a footbridge to this day.

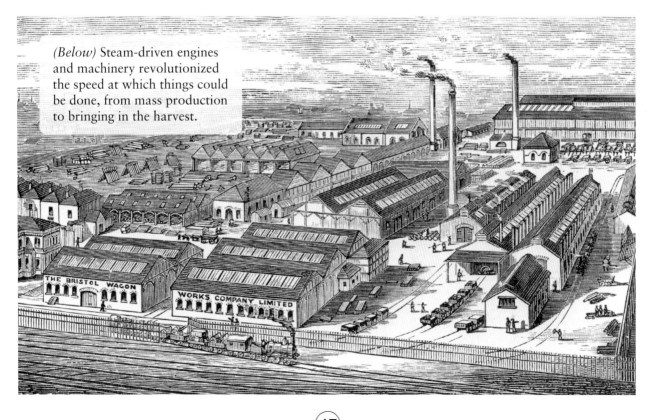

(Below) Steam-driven engines and machinery revolutionized the speed at which things could be done, from mass production to bringing in the harvest.

(Below) The amazing changes brought about by the use of metal in machines is shown in this historic railroad. The entire engine is made of metal, as are the tracks and the supports for the tressle bridge. Only the sleepers on the track and the upper framework of the carriages are made of wood. In the inset picture you can see how the use of traction engines allowed people to transport large quantities of goods across rough terrain, which would have been impossible before.

As steel became plentiful, it replaced wrought iron for almost all uses. With a lower price, people began to think how they might find new uses for metals. One of the most important was in the building industry.

At this time no one had developed alloy steels—those that are harder or more resistant to corrosion than mild steel. That needed another kind of furnace, one that did not use coke but electricity. It was called the electric arc furnace. The electric arc furnace was first demonstrated in 1879 by Sir William Siemens and was quickly put into widespread use to produce better-quality metals.

(Above) Metalworking was still a very labor-intensive industry throughout the 19th century.

The development of metal machines

The increase in iron making using coke meant there was growth in the demand for coal. As coal mines were made deeper, the mines flooded more easily. The solution was to produce a mechanical pump—one run by steam but, just as importantly, made of metal. It was invented in 1698 by Thomas Savery and was developed by Thomas Newcomen, and then, most extensively, by James Watt over the next century. The pump at first was partly made of wood but eventually was made entirely of iron.

The steam engine then allowed the building of other metal machines, which had previously been impossible to power. One example was the rolling mill, which could make iron bars, girders, and so on.

By 1812 trains were running on experimental track, with the first commercial railroad between Stockton and Darlington in England opening in 1825. As the railroad age began, the demand for iron and then steel for rails became enormous. There was also demand for iron and steel for railroad engines and carriages.

Toward the end of the 19th century the first internal combustion engines were invented. The blanks for engines were made of cast iron. Car bodies at first were wood, but very quickly they became pressed steel. So began the car industry, today one of the major consumers of the world's steel.

(Below) Metals revolutionized the way people lived during the Industrial Revolution. There were cheap metal pots and pans, and even metal baths. Cooking pots were often enameled iron. Stoves were made of cast iron instead of ceramic.

The modern metal age

Iron and steel dominated the 18th and 19th centuries. By the second half of the 19th century it was the turn of the chemists to lead the way, in particular through the development of the periodic table of the elements (see page 8). The periodic table put all of the known elements into a pattern and showed where there were elements still to find. Many of these elements were metals.

At this time, therefore, scientists knew about many metals, but most could not be extracted from their rocks on a large scale. Aluminum and magnesium were two of these metals. Aluminum is the most widespread metal in nature, but its use remained elusive because of the complexity of extraction. Like alloy steel, the process for its manufacture needed electricity. The method was developed in 1886 by Charles M. Hall in the United States and by Paul-Louis-Toussaint Héroult in France. At first, the aluminum produced was still the most expensive metal in the world, and it was even used for jewelry. However, with new electric processes to extract it from its ore, the price fell dramatically. As a result, people began to look for new uses for a material that was light, strong, and did not rust. Today aluminum is one of the most commonly used metals.

(Below) Aluminum, so widely used today, was still regarded as a precious metal and used for jewelry until the end of the 19th century, when Charles M. Hall *(above right)* and Paul-Louis-Toussaint Héroult *(above left)* invented a process for recovering it from bauxite by electrochemical means. Now it is produced on a massive scale. As production increased, the price fell. In recent years, for example, it has proved cheaper to make beverage containers from aluminum than to make them from glass.

With increasing understanding of the properties of metals, more and more of them have been put to good use, most especially as alloying metals combined with more common and traditional metals such as steel and aluminum. For example, titanium was, like aluminum, at first a curiosity rather than a practical metal. All this changed with the invention of a new way of extraction in 1950.

(Below) By the middle of the 20th century both machines and tools were made entirely from metal. As a result, productivity soared.

Pure titanium is easily bent and lies between aluminum and iron in density. However, when added to other metals, it can dramatically improve their corrosion resistance and strength. Titanium as a base metal is also widely used where lightness and corrosion resistance are important. It is used in aircraft, spacecraft, for artificial limb joints, and even for the casing of some portable computers.

(Below) Titanium is used as a coating on some drill bits to increase their efficiency.

(Above) Metals have been developed for many specialized purposes. This dentist's needle, for example, is made of titanium. Previously, needles were made of steel, and they had a tendency to snap inside the patient. The titanium ones do not snap; they just bend.

Joining metals

It is not enough to make metals. A way also has to be found to join pieces together. One way is to use RIVETS—short bars of material that are forced through holes in the pieces to be attached and then burred over at both ends.

By the end of the 19th century it became possible to use a combination of acetylene and oxygen gases to produce a flame that was hot enough to make iron and steel melt. As a result, it was possible to join these metals directly, a process called WELDING.

By 1902 electric arcs were also in use to weld metals. Electric arc welding is now the most common type used, for example, throughout the car industry.

(Above) Rivets are used to bind together metal sheets. They are hammered over when hot; and as they shrink on cooling, they grip the plates tightly.

(Below) Robot welders on a car production line.

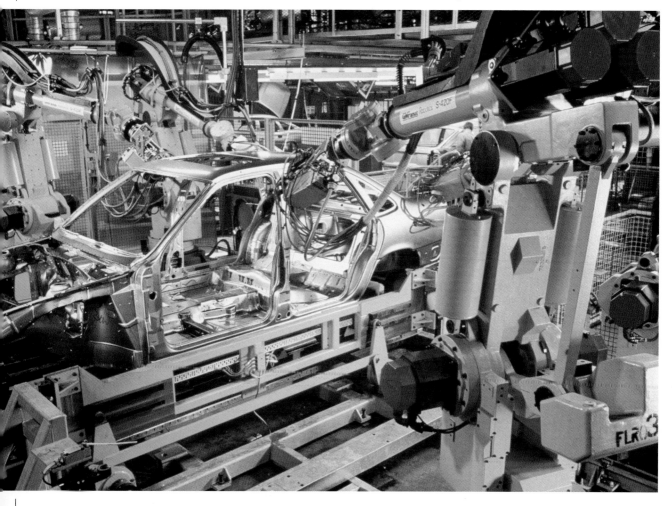

Metals and electricity

The Industrial Revolution was an age of iron and steel. The arrival of electricity brought some old metals, such as copper, as well as new ones, such as aluminum, to the fore.

Electricity is carried from power plants to homes, offices, and factories through wires. The best conductor for this purpose is copper. Copper is also malleable and so is good for flexible wiring. It is still used for internal wires such as those linking a computer to the wall socket and the wire connecting the socket to the main meter. For long-distance wiring, however, aluminum, which is nearly as good a conductor, is used because it is cheaper and lighter.

As electrical supply grew, so did the demand for copper and aluminum. But the electric age demanded even wider use of metals. For example, filaments for light bulbs and heating elements for stoves are often made of tungsten. In fact, for electric and electronic uses there is almost no limit to the number of metals applied. Many of these metals are available in very small amounts, so techniques had to be found for extracting them.

(Below) Tall utility towers, or pylons, of steel carrying high-voltage aluminum wires.

(Above) Aluminum is used for most long-distance electric wires.

(Below) A lithium battery is just one of the many innovations with metals. Lithium batteries have more power and retain a constant voltage for much longer than lead batteries.

The result of the widening of the scope of metals has meant that people have increasingly found uses for many previously unavailable metals, whether it be titanium for the cases of portable computers and artificial hip joints or the rare earth metals that are used in photoelectric cells.

Metals in buildings

Metals were not the first materials that people chose for making buildings. After all, metals have to be obtained by a long and complicated process of heating and then separating them from their rocks. Most people made buildings from mud, brick, stone, and timber. So it was not until the Industrial Revolution, beginning at the start of the 18th century, that metals began to play a major role in changing the way we build.

Using iron as a structural material took much development. At first, cast iron was used. Much ironwork from the Victorian Age (late 19th century) is cast iron, serving both to support buildings such as railroad stations and to add decoration.

Iron quickly became the fashionable as well as practical material for building. Solid columns of iron supported the upper roofs of warehouses and railroad stations where stone would previously have appeared.

As though to symbolize the achievements with iron and steel, in 1889 the crowning glory of the Paris Exposition was the 300-meter Eiffel Tower, built entirely of steel girders in the form of trusses. In the same exposition a glass and steel gallery to house an exhibition of machines covered nearly 49,000 square meters of space. It was so big that no other use could be found for it, and a gallery so big has never since been constructed.

See **Vol. 4: Ceramics** *for more on building materials.*

(Below) The Eiffel Tower, Paris, France.

(Below) Massive modern construction with metal trusses. The Sydney Harbor Bridge, Australia.

Metal makes strong frames

Many designs need to be strong and rigid. One way to do this, and to keep materials to the minimum, was invented about 2500 B.C., during the Bronze Age. They made frames using straight pieces of material shaped into triangles. Each piece used to make the triangle is called a truss.

The first trusses were made of wood and used to hold up roofs. But trusses can be made thinner and even stronger with metal. The Romans were the first to make metal trusses. They used bronze because at that time they could not work with iron and steel.

The main advances in metal trusses came in the late 18th and 19th century, when bridges were made first of cast and wrought iron and then later of steel. Cranes and many pieces of machinery have trusses as a way of combining strength and lightness.

Metal was preferred to wood in building construction for fire safety reasons as well as for strength. Fire was a constant hazard in factories because they were lighted with candles and later with gas. But above all, the use of metal frames allowed buildings to get taller. Textile mills could not have grown to six or seven stories in height without metal supports. In this case hollow columns supported the floors and were joined by bars of cast iron. Once the frame was built, the outer brick walls could easily be constructed.

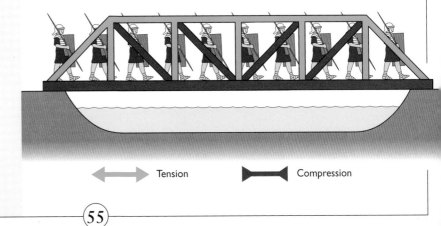

→← Tension   ►◄ Compression

See **Vol. 5: Glass** *for more on glass and the Crystal Palace in London.*

In early designs the iron frame and the brick supported one another. But as time went on, the iron frame was designed to be completely self-supporting. The biggest achievement here occurred in the early 20th century with the rise of the skyscraper. But before it there were spectacular iron-frame buildings such as the Crystal Palace built in London for the Great Exhibition of 1851 and made of cast iron and glass. It was high enough to completely enclose fully grown trees.

It was 564 meters long and made of prefabricated parts that were simply bolted together on site. As a result, all 90,000 square meters of space were covered in just six months.

Other forms of metal had equally dramatic, although not as spectacular, results. In the 1830s nails were made in bulk for the first time. This, too, reduced the cost of constructing buildings. Many 19th-century buildings in the United States used readily available timber fastened together with the revolutionary mass-produced nails. That allowed buildings to go up rapidly at a time when America was growing through massive immigration and expansion westward.

Metal was first made into room heaters in the 16th century. Wood- and coal-burning stoves were put in the center of a room to produce direct heating without an open fire. But James Watt had already thought of central heating, and by 1784 his office was heated by steam flowing through pipes. From these early beginnings modern central heating systems, with their copper pipes and steel radiators and boiler, developed. They not only made for better heating but, by taking open fires out of many rooms, greatly increased the safety of buildings.

Bathroom mechanisms were invented in 1778, and by this time all baths, sinks, and boilers for water were also made from metal—usually galvanized iron. Although sinks later changed to porcelain, porcelain baths were too brittle, so enameled cast-iron baths are still common. At the same time, metal faucets were introduced, along with metal door handles.

The first building with an all-metal structure was built in 1885 in Chicago—the 10-story Home Insurance Company Building. It began a rush to build higher and higher office blocks, all with a framework of steel holding them up. The electric elevator was invented by Elisha Otis using steel cables and an all-metal car. This made it possible to reach high floors in even taller buildings. In 1931 the skyscraper reached the unbelievable height of 102 stories and 381 meters in the construction of the Empire State Building.

Steel was also used for bridges, both when supported from below on girders and when hung from cables, such as the Brooklyn Bridge and the Golden Gate Bridge. Steel is also used in buildings where a large open space is needed. Today's warehouses are almost always made of a welded steel design that allows room for machines to move around inside them.

(Left and below) The Golden Gate Bridge, San Francisco, an example of a suspension bridge with metal cables and trusses to support the roadway.

(Below) The construction of the Empire State Building would not have been possible without metal frames.

Set Glossary

ACID RAIN: Rain that falls after having been contaminated by acid gases produced by power plants, vehicle exhausts, and other man-made sources.

ACIDITY: The tendency of a liquid to behave like an acid, reacting with metals and alkalis.

ADDITION POLYMERIZATION: The building blocks of many plastics (or polymers) are simple molecules called monomers. Monomers can be converted into polymers by making the monomers link to one another to form long chains in head-to-tail fashion. This is called addition polymerization or chain polymerization. It is most often used to link vinyl monomers to produce, for example, PVC, or polyvinyl chloride polymer.
See also **CONDENSATION POLYMERIZATION**

ADHESIVE: Any substance that can hold materials together simply by using some kind of surface attachment. In some cases this is a chemical reaction; in other cases it is a physical attraction between molecules of the adhesive and molecules of the substance it sticks to.

ADOBE: Simple unbaked brick made with mud, straw, and dung. It is dried in the open air. In this form it is very vulnerable to the effects of rainfall and so is most often found in desert areas or alternatively is protected by some waterproof covering, for example, thatch, straw, or reeds.

ALKALI: A base, or substance that can neutralize acids. In glassmaking an alkali is usually potassium carbonate and used as a flux to lower the melting point of the silica.

ALKYD: Any kind of synthetic resin used for protective coatings such as paint.

ALLOY: A metal mixture made up of two or more elements. Most of the elements used to make an alloy are metals. For example, brass is an alloy of copper and zinc, but carbon is an exception and used to make steel from iron.

AMALGAM: An alloy of mercury and one or more other metals. Dentist's filling amalgam traditionally contains mercury, silver, and tin.

AMPHIBIOUS: Adapted to function on both water and land.

AMORPHOUS: Shapeless and having no crystalline form. Glass is an amorphous solid.

ANION: An ion with a negative charge.

ANNEALING: A way of making a metal, alloy, or glass less brittle and more easy to work (more ductile) by heating it to a certain temperature (depending on the metal), holding it at that temperature for a certain time, and then cooling to room temperature.

ANODIZING: A method of plating metal by electrically depositing an oxide film onto the surface of a metal. The main purpose is to reduce corrosion.

ANTICYCLONE: A region of the Earth's atmosphere where the pressure is greater than average.

AQUEOUS SOLUTION: A substance dissolved in water.

ARTIFACT: An object of a previous time that was created by humans.

ARTIFICIAL DYE: A dye made from a chemical reaction that does not occur in nature. Dyes made from petroleum products are artificial dyes.

ARTIFICIAL FIBER: A fiber made from a material that has been manufactured, and that does not occur naturally. Rayon is an example of an artificial fiber.
Compare to **SYNTHETIC**

ATMOSPHERE: The envelope of gases that surrounds the Earth.

ATOM: The smallest particle of an element; a nucleus and its surrounding electrons.

AZO: A chemical compound that contains two nitrogen atoms joined by a double bond and each linked to a carbon atom. Azon compounds make up more than half of all dyes.

BARK: The exterior protective sheath of the stem and root of a woody plant such as a tree or a shrub. Everything beyond the cambium layer.

BAROMETER: An instrument for measuring atmospheric pressure.

BASE METAL: Having a low value and poorer properties than some other metals. Used, for example, when describing coins that contain metals other than gold or silver.

BAST FIBERS: A strong woody fiber that comes from the phloem of plants and is used for rope and similar products. Flax is an example of a bast fiber.

BATCH: A mixture of raw materials or products that are processes in a tank or kiln. This process produces small amounts of material or products and can be contrasted to continuous processes. Batch processing is used to make metals, alloys, glass, plastics, bricks, and other ceramics, dyes, and adhesives.

BAUXITE: A hydrated impure oxide of aluminum. It is the main ore used to obtain aluminum metal. The reddish-brown color of bauxite is caused by impurities of iron oxides.

BINDER: A substance used to make sure the pigment in a paint sticks to the surface it is applied to.

BIOCERAMICS: Ceramic materials that are used for medical and dental purposes, mainly as implants and replacements.

BLAST FURNACE: A tall furnace charged with a mixture of iron ore, coke, and limestone and used for the refining (smelting) of iron ore. The name comes from the strong blast of air used during smelting.

BLOWING: Forming a glass object by blowing into a gob of molten glass to form a bubble on the end of a blowpipe.

BOLL: The part of the cotton seed that contains the cotton fiber.

BOILING POINT: The temperature at which a liquid changes to a vapor. Boiling points change with atmospheric pressure.

BOND: A transfer or a sharing of electrons by two or more atoms. There are a number of kinds of chemical bonds, some very strong, such as covalent bonding and ionic bonding, and others quite weak, as in hydrogen bonding. Chemical bonds form because the linked molecules are more stable than the unlinked atoms from which they are formed.

BOYLE'S LAW: At constant temperature and for a given mass of gas the volume of the gas is inversely proportional to the pressure that builds up.

BRITTLE: Something that has almost no plasticity and so shatters rather than bends when a force is applied.

BULL'S EYE: A piece of glass with concentric rings marking the place where the blowpipe was attached to the glass. It is the central part of a pane of crown glass.

BUOYANCY: The tendency of an object to float if it is less dense than the liquid it is placed in.

BURN: A combustion reaction in which a flame is produced. A flame occurs where gases combust and release heat and light. At least two gases are therefore required if there is to be a flame.

CALORIFIC: Relating to the production of heat.

CAMBIUM: A thin growing layer that separates the xylem and phloem in most plants, and that produces new cell layers.

CAPACITOR: An electronic device designed for the temporary storage of electricity.

CAPILLARY ACTION, CAPILLARITY: The process by which surface tension forces can draw a liquid up a fine-bore tube.

CARBOHYDRATES: One of the main constituents of green plants, containing compounds of carbon, hydrogen, and oxygen. The main kinds of carbohydrate are sugars, starches, and celluloses.

CARBON COMPOUNDS: Any compound that includes the element carbon. Carbon compounds are also called organic compounds because they form an essential part of all living organisms.

CARBON CYCLE: The continuous movement of carbon between living things, the soil, the atmosphere, oceans, and rocks, especially those containing coal and petroleum.

CAST: To pour a liquid metal, glass, or other material into a mold and allow it to cool so that it solidifies and takes on the shape of the mold.

CATALYST: A substance that speeds up a chemical reaction but itself remains unchanged. For example, platinum is used in a catalytic converter of gases in the exhausts leaving motor vehicles.

CATALYTIC EFFECT: The way a substance helps speed up a reaction even though that substance does not form part of the reaction.

CATHODIC PROTECTION: The technique of protecting a metal object by connecting it to a more easily oxidizable material. The metal object being protected is made into the cathode of a cell. For example, iron can be protected by coupling it with magnesium.

CATION: An ion with a positive charge, often a metal.

CELL: A vessel containing two electrodes and a liquid substance that conducts electricity (an electrolyte).

CELLULOSE: A form of carbohydrate. *See* **CARBOHYDRATE**

CEMENT: A mixture of alumina, silica, lime, iron oxide, and magnesium oxide that is burned together in a kiln and then made into a powder. It is used as the main ingredient of mortar and as the adhesive in concrete.

CERAMIC: A crystalline nonmetal. In a more everyday sense it is a material based on clay that has been heated so that it has chemically hardened.

CHARRING: To burn partly so that some of a material turns to carbon and turns black.

CHINA: A shortened version of the original "Chinese porcelain," it also refers to various porcelain objects such as plates and vases meant for domestic use.

CHINA CLAY: The mineral kaolinite, which is a very white clay used as the basis of porcelain manufacture.

CLAY MINERALS: The minerals, such as kaolinite, illite, and montmorillonite, that occur naturally in soils and some rocks, and that are all minute platelike crystals.

COKE: A form of coal that has been roasted in the absence of air to remove much of the liquid and gas content.

COLORANTS: Any substance that adds a color to a material. The pigments in paints and the chemicals that make dyes are colorants.

COLORFAST: A dye that will not "run" in water or change color when it is exposed to sunlight.

COMPOSITE MATERIALS: Materials such as plywood that are normally regarded as a single material, but that themselves are made up of a number of different materials bonded together.

COMPOUND: A chemical consisting of two or more elements chemically bonded together, for example, calcium carbonate.

COMPRESSED AIR: Air that has been squashed to reduce its volume.

COMPRESSION: To be squashed.

COMPRESSION MOLDING: The shaping of an object, such as a headlight lens, which is achieved by squashing it into a mold.

CONCRETE: A mixture of cement and a coarse material such as sand and small stones.

CONDENSATION: The process of changing a gas to a liquid.

CONDENSATION POLYMERIZATION: The production of a polymer formed by a chain of reactions in which a water molecule is eliminated as every link of the polymer is formed. Polyester is an example.

CONDUCTION: (i) The exchange of heat (heat conduction) by contact with another object, or (ii) allowing the flow of electrons (electrical conduction).

CONDUCTIVITY: The property of allowing the flow of heat or electricity.

CONDUCTOR: (i) Heat—a material that allows heat to flow in and out of it easily. (ii) Electricity—a material that allows electrons to flow through it easily.

CONTACT ADHESIVE: An adhesive that, when placed on the surface to be joined, sticks as soon as the surfaces are placed firmly together.

CONVECTION: The circulating movement of molecules in a liquid or gas as a result of heating it from below.

CORRODE/CORROSION: A reaction usually between a metal and an acid or alkali in which the metal decomposes. The word is used in the sense of the metal being eaten away and dangerously thinned.

CORROSIVE: Causing corrosion, that is, the oxidation of a metal. For example, sodium hydroxide is corrosive.

COVALENT BONDING: The most common type of strong chemical bond, which occurs when two atoms share electrons. For example, oxygen O_2.

CRANKSHAFT: A rodlike piece of a machine designed to change linear into rotational motion or vice versa.

CRIMP: To cause to become wavy.

CRUCIBLE: A ceramic-lined container for holding molten metal, glass, and so on.

CRUDE OIL: A chemical mixture of petroleum liquids. Crude oil forms the raw material for an oil refinery.

CRYSTAL: A substance that has grown freely so that it can develop external faces.

CRYSTALLINE: A solid in which the atoms, ions, or molecules are organized into an orderly pattern without distinct crystal faces.

CURING: The process of allowing a chemical change to occur simply by waiting a while. Curing is often a process of reaction with water or with air.

CYLINDER GLASS: An old method of making window glass by blowing a large bubble of glass, then swinging it until it forms a cylinder. The ends of the cylinder are then cut off with shears and the sides of the cylinder allowed to open out until they form a flat sheet.

DECIDUOUS: A plant that sheds its leaves seasonally.

DECOMPOSE: To rot. Decomposing plant matter releases nutrients back to the soil and in this way provides nourishment for a new generation of living things.

DENSITY: The mass per unit volume (for example, g/c^3).

DESICCATE: To dry up thoroughly.

DETERGENT: A cleaning agent that is able to turn oils and dirts into an emulsion and then hold them in suspension so they can be washed away.

DIE: A tool for giving metal a required shape either by striking the object with the die or by forcing the object over or through the die.

DIFFUSION: The slow mixing of one substance with another until the two substances are evenly mixed. Mixing occurs because of differences in concentration within the mixture. Diffusion works rapidly with gases, very slowly with liquids.

DILUTE: To add more of a solvent to a solution.

DISSOCIATE: To break up. When a compound dissociates, its molecules break up into separate ions.

DISSOLVED: To break down a substance in a solution without causing a reaction.

DISTILLATION: The process of separating mixtures by condensing the vapors through cooling. The simplest form of distillation uses a Liebig condenser arranged with just a slight slope down to the collecting vessel. When the liquid mixture is heated and vapors are produced, they enter the water cooled condenser and then flow down the tube, where they can be collected.

DISTILLED WATER: Water that has its dissolved solids removed by the process of distillation.

DOPING: Adding an impurity to the surface of a substance in order to change its properties.

DORMANT: A period of inactivity such as during winter, when plants stop growing.

DRAWING: The process in which a piece of metal is pulled over a former or through dies.

DRY-CLEANED: A method of cleaning fabrics with nonwater-based organic solvents such as carbon tetrachloride.

DUCTILE: Capable of being drawn out or hammered thin.

DYE: A colored substance that will stick to another substance so that both appear to be colored.

EARLY WOOD: The wood growth put on the spring of each year.

EARTHENWARE: Pottery that has not been fired to the point where some of the clay crystals begin to melt and fuse together and is thus slightly porous and coarser than stoneware or porcelain.

ELASTIC: The ability of an object to regain its original shape after it has been deformed.

ELASTIC CHANGE: To change shape elastically.

ELASTICITY: The property of a substance that causes it to return to its original shape after it has been deformed in some way.

ELASTIC LIMIT: The largest force that a material can stand before it changes shape permanently.

ELECTRODE: A conductor that forms one terminal of a cell.

ELECTROLYSIS: An electrical-chemical process that uses an electric current to cause the breakup of a compound and the movement of metal ions in a solution. It is commonly used in industry for purifying (refining) metals or for plating metal objects with a fine, even metal coat.

ELECTROLYTE: An ionic solution that conducts electricity.

ELECTROMAGNET: A temporary magnet that is produced when a current of electricity passes through a coil of wire.

ELECTRON: A tiny, negatively charged particle that is part of an atom. The flow of electrons through a solid material such as a wire produces an electric current.

ELEMENT: A substance that cannot be decomposed into simpler substances by chemical means, for example, silver and copper.

EMULSION: Tiny droplets of one substance dispersed in another.

EMULSION PAINT: A paint made of an emulsion that is water soluble (also called latex paint).

ENAMEL: A substance made of finely powdered glass colored with a metallic oxide and suspended in oil so that it can be applied with a brush. The enamel is then heated, the oil burns away, and the glass fuses. Also used colloquially to refer to certain kinds of resin-based paint that have extremely durable properties.

ENGINEERED WOOD PRODUCTS: Wood products such as plywood sheeting made from a combination of wood sheets, chips or sawdust, and resin.

EVAPORATION: The change of state of a liquid to a gas. Evaporation happens below the boiling point.

EXOTHERMIC REACTION: A chemical reaction that gives out heat.

EXTRUSION: To push a substance through an opening so as to change its shape.

FABRIC: A material made by weaving threads into a network, often just referred to as cloth.

FELTED: Wool that has been hammered in the presence of heat and moisture to change its texture and mat the fibers.

FERRITE: A magnetic substance made of ferric oxide combined with manganese, nickel, or zinc oxide.

FIBER: A long thread.

FILAMENT: (i) The coiled wire used inside a light bulb. It consists of a high-resistance metal such as tungsten that also has a high melting point. (ii) A continuous thread produced during the manufacture of fibers.

FILLER: A material introduced in order to give bulk to a substance. Fillers are used in making paper and also in the manufacture of paints and some adhesives.

FILTRATE: The liquid that has passed through a filter.

FLOOD: When rivers spill over their banks and cover the surrounding land with water.

FLUID: Able to flow either as a liquid or a gas.

FLUORESCENT: A substance that gives out visible light when struck by invisible waves, such as ultraviolet rays.

FLUX: A substance that lowers the melting temperature of another substance. Fluxes are use in glassmaking and in melting alloys. A flux is used, for example, with a solder.

FORMER: An object used to control the shape or size of a product being made, for example, glass.

FOAM: A material that is sufficiently gelatinous to be able to contain bubbles of gas. The gas bulks up the substances, making it behave as though it were semirigid.

FORGE: To hammer a piece of heated metal until it changes to the desired shape.

FRACTION: A group of similar components of a mixture. In the petroleum industry the light fractions of crude oil are those with the smallest molecules, while the medium and heavy fractions have larger molecules.

FRACTIONAL DISTILLATION: The separation of the components of a liquid mixture by heating them to their boiling points.

FREEZING POINT: The temperature at which a substance undergoes a phase change from a liquid to a solid. It is the same temperature as the melting point.

FRIT: Partly fused materials of which glass is made.

FROTH SEPARATION: A process in which air bubbles are blown through a suspension, causing a froth of bubbles to collect on the surface. The materials that are attracted to the bubbles can then be removed with the froth.

FURNACE: An enclosed fire designed to produce a very high degree of heat for melting glass or metal or for reheating objects so they can be further processed.

FUSING: The process of melting particles of a material so they form a continuous sheet or solid object. Enamel is bonded to the surface of glass this way. Powder-formed metal is also fused into a solid piece. Powder paints are fused to the surface by heating.

GALVANIZING: The application of a surface coating of zinc to iron or steel.

GAS: A form of matter in which the molecules take no definite shape and are free to move around to uniformly fill any vessel they are put in. A gas can easily be compressed into a much smaller volume.

GIANT MOLECULES: Molecules that have been formed by polymerization.

GLASS: A homogeneous, often transparent material with a random noncrystalline molecular structure. It is achieved by cooling a molten substance very rapidly so that it cannot crystallize.

GLASS CERAMIC: A ceramic that is not entirely crystalline.

GLASSY STATE: A solid in which the molecules are arranged randomly rather than being formed into crystals.

GLOBAL WARMING: The progressive increase in the average temperature of the Earth's atmosphere, most probably in large part due to burning fossil fuels.

GLUE: An adhesive made from boiled animal bones.

GOB: A piece of near-molten glass used by glass-blowers and in machines to make hollow glass vessels.

GRAIN: (i) The distinctive pattern of fibers in wood. (ii) Small particles of a solid, including a single crystal.

GRAPHITE: A form of the element carbon with a sheetlike structure.

GRAVITY: The attractive force produced because of the mass of an object.

GREENHOUSE EFFECT: An increase in the global air temperature as a result of heat released from burning fossil fuels being absorbed by carbon dioxide in the atmosphere.

GREENHOUSE GAS: Any of various gases that contribute to the greenhouse effect, such as carbon dioxide.

GROUNDWATER: Water that flows naturally through rocks as part of the water cycle.

GUM: Any natural adhesive of plant origin that consists of colloidal polysaccharide substances that are gelatinous when moist but harden on drying.

HARDWOOD: The wood from a nonconiferous tree.

HEARTWOOD: The old, hard, nonliving central wood of trees.

HEAT: The energy that is transferred when a substance is at a different temperature than that of its surroundings.

HEAT CAPACITY: The ratio of the heat supplied to a substance compared with the rise in temperature that is produced.

HOLOGRAM: A three-dimensional image reproduced from a split laser beam.

HYDRATION: The process of absorption of water by a substance. In some cases hydration makes a substance change color, but in all cases there is a change in volume.

HYDROCARBON: A compound in which only hydrogen and carbon atoms are present. Most fuels are hydrocarbons, for example, methane.

HYDROFLUORIC ACID: An extremely corrosive acid that attacks silicate minerals such as glass. It is used to etch decoration onto glass and also to produce some forms of polished surface.

HYDROGEN BOND: A type of attractive force that holds one molecule to another. It is one of the weaker forms of intermolecular attractive force.

HYDROLYSIS: A reversible process of decomposition of a substance in water.

HYDROPHILIC: Attracted to water.

HYDROPHOBIC: Repelled by water.

IMMISCIBLE: Will not mix with another substance, for example, oil and water.

IMPURITIES: Any substances that are found in small quantities, and that are not meant to be in the solution or mixture.

INCANDESCENT: Glowing with heat, for example, a tungsten filament in a light bulb.

INDUSTRIAL REVOLUTION: The time, which began in the 18th century and continued through into the 19th century, when materials began to be made with the use of power machines and mass production.

INERT: A material that does not react chemically.

INORGANIC: A substance that does not contain the element carbon (and usually hydrogen), for example, sodium chloride.

INSOLUBLE: A substance that will not dissolve, for example, gold in water.

INSULATOR: A material that does not conduct electricity.

ION: An atom or group of atoms that has gained or lost one or more electrons and so developed an electrical charge.

IONIC BONDING: The form of bonding that occurs between two ions when the ions have opposite charges, for example, sodium ions bond with chloride ions to make sodium chloride. Ionic bonds are strong except in the presence of a solvent.

IONIZE: To change into ions.

ISOTOPE: An atom that has the same number of protons in its nucleus, but that has a different mass, for example, carbon 12 and carbon 14.

KAOLINITE: A form of clay mineral found concentrated as china clay. It is the result of the decomposition of the mineral feldspar.

KILN: An oven used to heat materials. Kilns at quite low temperatures are used to dry wood and at higher temperatures to bake bricks and to fuse enamel onto the surfaces of other substances. They are a form of furnace.

KINETIC ENERGY: The energy due to movement. When a ball is thrown, it has kinetic energy.

KNOT: The changed pattern in rings in wood due to the former presence of a branch.

LAMINATE: An engineered wood product consisting of several wood layers bonded by a resin. Also applies to strips of paper stuck together with resins to make such things as "formica" worktops.

LATE WOOD: Wood produced during the summer part of the growing season.

LATENT HEAT: The amount of heat that is absorbed or released during the process of changing state between gas, liquid, or solid. For example, heat is absorbed when liquid changes to gas. Heat is given out again as the gas condenses back to a liquid.

LATEX: A general term for a colloidal suspension of rubber-type material in water. Originally for the milky white liquid emulsion found in the Para rubber tree, but also now any manufactured water emulsion containing synthetic rubber or plastic.

LATEX PAINT: A water emulsion of a synthetic rubber or plastic used as paint.
See **EMULSION PAINT**

LATHE: A tool consisting of a rotating spindle and cutters that is designed to produce shaped objects that are symmetrical about the axis of rotation.

LATTICE: A regular geometric arrangement of objects in space.

LEHR: The oven used for annealing glassware. It is usually a very long tunnel through which glass passes on a conveyor belt.

LIGHTFAST: A colorant that does not fade when exposed to sunlight.

LIGNIN: A form of hard cellulose that forms the walls of cells.

LIQUID: A form of matter that has a fixed volume but no fixed shape.

LUMBER: Timber that has been dressed for use in building or carpentry and consists of planed planks.

MALLEABLE: Capable of being hammered or rolled into a new shape without fracturing due to brittleness.

MANOMETER: A device for measuring liquid or gas pressure.

MASS: The amount of matter in an object. In common use the word weight is used instead (incorrectly) to mean mass.

MATERIAL: Anything made of matter.

MATTED: Another word for felted.
See **FELTED**

MATTER: Anything that has mass and takes up space.

MELT: The liquid glass produced when a batch of raw materials melts. Also used to describe molten metal.

MELTING POINT: The temperature at which a substance changes state from a solid phase to a liquid phase. It is the same as the freezing point.

METAL: A class of elements that is a good conductor of electricity and heat, has a metallic luster, is malleable and ductile, and is formed as cations held together by a sea of electrons. A metal may also be an alloy of these elements and carbon.

METAL FATIGUE: The gradual weakening of a metal by constant bending until a crack develops.

MINERAL: A solid substance made of just one element or compound, for example, calcite minerals contain only calcium carbonate.

MISCIBLE: Capable of being mixed.

MIXTURE: A material that can be separated into two or more substances using physical means, for example, air.

MOLD: A containing shape made of wood, metal, or sand into which molten glass or metal is poured. In metalworking it produces a casting. In glassmaking the glass is often blown rather than poured when making, for example, light bulbs.

MOLECULE: A group of two or more atoms held together by chemical bonds.

MONOMER: A small molecule and building block for larger chain molecules or polymers (mono means "one" and mer means "part").

MORDANT: A chemical that is attracted to a dye and also to the surface that is to be dyed.

MOSAIC: A decorated surface made from a large number of small colored pieces of glass, natural stone, or ceramic that are cemented together.

NATIVE METAL: A pure form of a metal not combined as a compound. Native metals are more common in nonreactive elements such as gold than reactive ones such as calcium.

NATURAL DYES: Dyes made from plants without any chemical alteration, for example, indigo.

NATURAL FIBERS: Fibers obtained from plants or animals, for example, flax and wool.

NEUTRON: A particle inside the nucleus of an atom that is neutral and has no charge.

NOBLE GASES: The members of group 8 of the periodic table of the elements: helium, neon, argon, krypton, xenon, radon. These gases are almost entirely unreactive.

NONMETAL: A brittle substance that does not conduct electricity, for example, sulfur or nitrogen.

OIL-BASED PAINTS: Paints that are not based on water as a vehicle. Traditional artists' oil paint uses linseed oil as a vehicle.

OPAQUE: A substance through which light cannot pass.

ORE: A rock containing enough of a useful substance to make mining it worthwhile, for example, bauxite, the ore of aluminum.

ORGANIC: A substance that contains carbon and usually hydrogen. The carbonates are usually excluded.

OXIDE: A compound that includes oxygen and one other element, for example, Cu_2O, copper oxide.

OXIDIZE, OXIDIZING AGENT: A reaction that occurs when a substance combines with oxygen or a reaction in which an atom, ion, or molecule loses electrons to another substance (and in this more general case does not have to take up oxygen).

OZONE: A form of oxygen whose molecules contain three atoms of oxygen. Ozone high in the atmosphere blocks harmful ultraviolet rays from the Sun, but at ground level it is an irritant gas when breathed in and so is regarded as a form of pollution. The ozone layer is the uppermost part of the stratosphere.

PAINT: A coating that has both decorative and protective properties, and that consists of a pigment suspended in a vehicle, or binder, made of a resin dissolved in a solvent. It dries to give a tough film.

PARTIAL PRESSURE: The pressure a gas in a mixture would exert if it alone occupied the flask. For example, oxygen makes up about a fifth of the atmosphere. Its partial pressure is therefore about a fifth of normal atmospheric pressure.

PASTE: A thick suspension of a solid in a liquid.

PATINA: A surface coating that develops on metals and protects them from further corrosion, for example, the green coating of copper carbonate that forms on copper statues.

PERIODIC TABLE: A chart organizing elements by atomic number and chemical properties into groups and periods.

PERMANENT HARDNESS: Hardness in the water that cannot be removed by boiling.

PETROCHEMICAL: Any of a large group of manufactured chemicals (not fuels) that come from petroleum and natural gas. It is usually taken to include similar products that can be made from coal and plants.

PETROLEUM: A natural mixture of a range of gases, liquids, and solids derived from the decomposed remains of animals and plants.

PHASE: A particular state of matter. A substance can exist as a solid, liquid, or gas and may change between these phases with the addition or removal of energy, usually in the form of heat.

PHOSPHOR: A material that glows when energized by ultraviolet or electron beams, such as in fluorescent tubes and cathode ray tubes.

PHOTOCHEMICAL SMOG: A mixture of tiny particles of dust and soot combined with a brown haze caused by the reaction of colorless nitric oxide from vehicle exhausts and oxygen of the air to form brown nitrogen dioxide.

PHOTOCHROMIC GLASSES: Glasses designed to change color with the intensity of light. They use the property that certain substances, for example, silver halide, can change color (and change chemically) in light. For example, when silver chromide is dispersed in the glass melt, sunlight decomposes the silver halide to release silver (and so darken the lens). But the halogen cannot escape; and when the light is removed, the halogen recombines with the silver to turn back to colorless silver halide.

PHOTOSYNTHESIS: The natural process that happens in green plants whereby the energy from light is used to help turn gases, water, and minerals into tissue and energy.

PIEZOELECTRICS: Materials that produce electric currents when they are deformed, or vice versa.

PIGMENT: Insoluble particles of coloring material.

PITH: The central strand of spongy tissue found in the stems of most plants.

PLASTIC: Material—a carbon-based substance consisting of long chains or networks (polymers) of simple molecules. The word plastic is commonly used only for synthetic polymers. Property—a material is plastic if it can be made to change shape easily and then remain in this new shape (contrast with elasticity and brittleness).

PLASTIC CHANGE: A permanent change in shape that happens without breaking.

PLASTICIZER: A chemical added to rubbers and resins to make it easier for them to be deformed and molded. Plasticizers are also added to cement to make it more easily worked when used as a mortar.

PLATE GLASS: Rolled, ground, and polished sheet glass.

PLIABLE: Supple enough to be repeatedly bent without fracturing.

PLYWOOD: An engineered wood laminate consisting of sheets of wood bonded with resin. Each sheet of wood has the grain at right angles to the one above and below. This imparts stability to the product.

PNEUMATIC DEVICE: Any device that works with air pressure.

POLAR: Something that has a partial electric charge.

POLYAMIDES: A compound that contains more than one amide group, for example, nylon.

POLYMER: A compound that is made of long chains or branching networks by combining molecules called monomers as repeating units. Poly means "many," mer means "part."

PORCELAIN: A hard, fine-grained, and translucent white ceramic that is made of china clay and is fired to a high temperature. Varieties include china.

PORES: Spaces between particles that are small enough to hold water by capillary action, but large enough to allow water to enter.

POROUS: A material that has small cavities in it, known as pores. These pores may or may not be joined. As a result, porous materials may or may not allow a liquid or gas to pass through them. Popularly, porous is used to mean permeable, the kind of porosity in which the pores are joined, and liquids or gases can flow.

POROUS CERAMICS: Ceramics that have not been fired at temperatures high enough to cause the clays to fuse and so prevent the slow movement of water.

POTENTIAL ENERGY: Energy due to the position of an object. Water in a reservoir has potential energy because it is stored up, and when released, it moves down to a lower level.

POWDER COATING: The application of a pigment in powder form without the use of a solvent.

POWDER FORMING: A process of using a powder to fill a mold and then heating the powder to make it fuse into a solid.

PRECIPITATE: A solid substance formed as a result of a chemical reaction between two liquids or gases.

PRESSURE: The force per unit area measured in SI units in Pascals and also more generally in atmospheres.

PRIMARY COLORS: A set of colors from which all others can be made. In transmitted light they are red, blue, and green.

PROTEIN: Substances in plants and animals that include nitrogen.

PROTON: A positively charged particle in the nucleus of an atom that balances out the charge of the surrounding electrons.

QUENCH: To put into water in order to cool rapidly.

RADIATION: The transmission of energy from one body to another without any contribution from the intervening space. *Contrast with* **CONVECTION** and **CONDUCTION**

RADIOACTIVE: A substance that spontaneously emits energetic particles.

RARE EARTHS: Any of a group of metal oxides that are found widely throughout the Earth's rocks, but in low concentrations. They are mainly made up of the elements of the lanthanide series of the periodic table of the elements.

RAW MATERIAL: A substance that has not been prepared, but that has an intended use in manufacturing.

RAY: Narrow beam of light.

RAYON: An artificial fiber made from natural cellulose.

REACTION (CHEMICAL): The recombination of two substances using parts of each substance.

REACTIVE: A substance that easily reacts with many other substances.

RECYCLE: To take once used materials and make them available for reuse.

REDUCTION, REDUCING AGENT: The removal of oxygen from or the addition of hydrogen to a compound.

REFINING: Separating a mixture into the simpler substances of which it is made, especially petrochemical refining.

REFRACTION: The bending of a ray of light as it passes between substances of different refractive index (light-bending properties).

REFRACTORY: Relating to the use of a ceramic material, especially a brick, in high-temperature conditions of, for example, a furnace.

REFRIGERANT: A substance that, on changing between a liquid and a gas, can absorb large amounts of (latent) heat from its surroundings.

REGENERATED FIBERS: Fibers that have been dissolved in a solution and then recovered from the solution in a different form.

REINFORCED FIBER: A fiber that is mixed with a resin, for example, glass-reinforced fiber.

RESIN: A semisolid natural material that is made of plant secretions and often yellow-brown in color. Also synthetic materials with the same type of properties. Synthetic resins have taken over almost completely from natural resins and are available as thermoplastic resins and thermosetting resins.

RESPIRATION: The process of taking in oxygen and releasing carbon dioxide in animals and the reverse in plants.

RIVET: A small rod of metal that is inserted into two holes in metal sheets and then burred over at both ends in order to stick the sheets together.

ROCK: A naturally hard inorganic material composed of mineral particles or crystals.

ROLLING: The process in which metal is rolled into plates and bars.

ROSIN: A brittle form of resin used in varnishes.

RUST: The product of the corrosion of iron and steel in the presence of air and water.

SALT: Generally thought of as sodium chloride, common salt; however, more generally a salt is a compound involving a metal. There are therefore many "salts" in water in addition to sodium chloride.

SAPWOOD: The outer, living layers of the tree, which includes cells for the transportation of water and minerals between roots and leaves.

SATURATED: A state in which a liquid can hold no more of a substance dissolved in it.

SEALANTS: A material designed to stop water or other liquids from penetrating into a surface or between surfaces. Most sealants are adhesives.

SEMICONDUCTOR: A crystalline solid that has an electrical conductivity part way between a conductor and an insulator. This material can be altered by doping to control an electric current. Semiconductors are the basis of transistors, integrated circuits, and other modern electronic solid-state devices.

SEMIPERMEABLE MEMBRANE: A thin material that acts as a fine sieve or filter, allowing small molecules to pass, but holding back large molecules.

SEPARATING COLUMN: A tall glass tube containing a porous disk near the base and filled with a substance such as aluminum oxide that can absorb materials on its surface. When a mixture passes through the columns, fractions are retarded by differing amounts so that each fraction is washed through the column in sequence.

SEPARATING FUNNEL: A pear-shaped glass funnel designed to permit the separation of immiscible liquids by simply pouring off the more dense liquid from the bottom of the funnel, while leaving the less dense liquid in the funnel.

SHAKES: A defect in wood produced by the wood tissue separating, usually parallel to the rings.

SHEEN: A lustrous, shiny surface on a yarn. It is produced by the finishing process or may be a natural part of the yarn.

SHEET-METAL FORMING: The process of rolling out metal into sheet.

SILICA: Silicon dioxide, most commonly in the form of sand.

SILICA GLASS: Glass made exclusively of silica.

SINTER: The process of heating that makes grains of a ceramic or metal a solid mass before it becomes molten.

SIZE: A glue, varnish, resin, or similar very dilute adhesive sealant used to block up the pores in porous surfaces or, for example, plaster and paper. Once the size has dried, paint or other surface coatings can be applied without the coating sinking in.

SLAG: A mixture of substances that are waste products of a furnace. Most slag are mainly composed of silicates.

SMELTING: Roasting a substance in order to extract the metal contained in it.

SODA: A flux for glassmaking consisting of sodium carbonate.

SOFTWOOD: Wood obtained from a coniferous tree.

SOLID: A rigid form of matter that maintains its shape regardless of whether or not it is in a container.

SOLIDIFICATION: Changing from a liquid to a solid.

SOLUBILITY: The maximum amount of a substance that can be contained in a solvent.

SOLUBLE: Readily dissolvable in a solvent.

SOLUTION: A mixture of a liquid (the solvent) and at least one other substance of lesser abundance (the solute). Like all mixtures, solutions can be separated by physical means.

SOLVAY PROCESS: Modern method of manufacturing the industrial alkali sodium carbonate (soda ash).

SOLVENT: The main substance in a solution.

SPECTRUM: A progressive series arranged in order, for example, the range of colors that make up visible light as seen in a rainbow.

SPINNERET: A small metal nozzle perforated with many small holes through which a filament solution is forced. The filaments that emerge are solidified by cooling and the filaments twisted together to form a yarn.

SPINNING: The process of drawing out and twisting short fibers, for example, wool, and thus making a thread or yarn.

SPRING: A natural flow of water from the ground.

STABILIZER: A chemical that, when added to other chemicals, prevents further reactions. For example, in soda lime glass the lime acts as a stabilizer for the silica.

STAPLE: A short fiber that has to be twisted with other fibers (spun) in order to make a long thread or yarn.

STARCHES: One form of carbohydrate. Starches can be used to make adhesives.

STATE OF MATTER: The physical form of matter. There are three states of matter: liquid, solid, and gas.

STEAM: Water vapor at the boiling point of water.

STONEWARE: Nonwhite pottery that has been fired at a high temperature until some of the clay has fused, a state called vitrified. Vitrification makes the pottery impervious to water. It is used for general tableware, often for breakfast crockery.

STRAND: When a number of yarns are twisted together, they make a strand. Strands twisted together make a rope.

SUBSTANCE: A type of material including mixtures.

SULFIDE: A compound that is composed only of metal and sulfur atoms, for example, PbS, the mineral galena.

SUPERCONDUCTORS: Materials that will conduct electricity with virtually no resistance if they are cooled to temperatures close to absolute zero (–273°C).

SURFACE TENSION: The force that operates on the surface of a liquid, and that makes it act as though it were covered with an invisible elastic film.

SURFACTANT: A substance that acts on a surface, such as a detergent.

SUSPENDED, SUSPENSION: Tiny particles in a liquid or a gas that do not settle out with time.

SYNTHETIC: Something that does not occur naturally but has to be manufactured. Synthetics are often produced from materials that do not occur in nature, for example, from petrochemicals. (i) Dye—a synthetic dye is made from petrochemicals, as opposed to natural dyes that are made of extracts of plants. (ii) Fiber—synthetic is a subdivision of artificial. Although both polyester and rayon are artificial fibers, rayon is made from reconstituted natural cellulose fibers and so is not synthetic, while polyester is made from petrochemicals and so is a synthetic fiber.

TANNIN: A group of pale-yellow or light-brown substances derived from plants that are used in dyeing fabric and making ink. Tannins are soluble in water and produce dark-blue or dark-green solutions when added to iron compounds.

TARNISH: A coating that develops as a result of the reaction between a metal and the substances in the air. The most common form of tarnishing is a very thin transparent oxide coating, such as occurs on aluminum. Sulfur compounds in the air make silver tarnish black.

TEMPER: To moderate or to make stronger: used in the metal industry to describe softening hardened steel or cast iron by reheating at a lower temperature or to describe hardening steel by reheating and cooling in oil; or in the glass industry, to describe toughening glass by first heating it and then slowly cooling it.

TEMPORARILY HARD WATER: Hard water that contains dissolved substances that can be removed by boiling.

TENSILE (PULLING STRENGTH): The greatest lengthwise (pulling) stress a substance can bear without tearing apart.

TENSION: A state of being pulled. Compare to compression.

TERRA COTTA: Red earth-colored glazed or unglazed fired clay whose origins lie in the Mediterranean region of Europe.

THERMOPLASTIC: A plastic that will soften and can be molded repeatedly into different shapes. It will then set into the molded shape as it cools.

THERMOSET: A plastic that will set into a molded shape as it first cools, but that cannot be made soft again by reheating.

THREAD: A long length of filament, group of filaments twisted together, or a long length of short fibers that have been spun and twisted together into a continuous strand.

TIMBER: A general term for wood suitable for building or for carpentry and consisting of roughcut planks. *Compare to* **LUMBER**

TRANSITION METALS: Any of the group of metallic elements (for example, chromium and iron) that belong to the central part of the periodic table of the elements and whose oxides commonly occur in a variety of colors.

TRANSPARENT: Something that will readily let light through, for example, window glass. Compare to translucent, when only some light gets through but an image cannot be seen, for example, greaseproof paper.

TROPOSPHERE: The lower part of the atmosphere in which clouds form. In general, temperature decreases with height.

TRUNK: The main stem of a tree.

VACUUM: Something from which all air has been removed.

VAPOR: The gaseous phase of a substance that is a liquid or a solid at that temperature, for example, water vapor is the gaseous form of water.

VAPORIZE: To change from a liquid to a gas, or vapor.

VENEER: A thin sheet of highly decorative wood that is applied to cheap wood or engineered wood products to improve their appearance and value.

VINYL: Often used as a general name for plastic. Strictly, vinyls are polymers derived from ethylene by removal of one hydrogen atom, for example, PVC, polyvinylchloride.

VISCOSE: A yellow-brown solution made by treating cellulose with alkali solution and carbon disulfide and used to make rayon.

VISCOUS, VISCOSITY: Sticky. Viscosity is a measure of the resistance of a liquid to flow. The higher the viscosity—the more viscous it is—the less easily it will flow.

VITREOUS CHINA: A translucent form of china or porcelain.

VITRIFICATION: To heat until a substance changes into a glassy form and fuses together.

VOLATILE: Readily forms a gas. Some parts of a liquid mixture are often volatile, as is the case for crude oil. This allows them to be separated by distillation.

WATER CYCLE: The continual interchange of water between the oceans, the air, clouds, rain, rivers, ice sheets, soil, and rocks.

WATER VAPOR: The gaseous form of water.

WAVELENGTH: The distance between adjacent crests on a wave. Shorter wavelengths have smaller distances between crests than longer wavelengths.

WAX: Substances of animal, plant, mineral, or synthetic origin that are similar to fats but are less greasy and harder. They form hard films that can be polished.

WEAVING: A way of making a fabric by passing two sets of yarns through one another at right angles to make a kind of tight meshed net with no spaces between the yarns.

WELDING: Technique used for joining metal pieces through intense localized heat. Welding often involves the use of a joining metal such as a rod of steel used to attach steel pieces (arc welding).

WETTING: In adhesive spreading, a term that refers to the complete coverage of an adhesive over a surface.

WETTING AGENT: A substance that is able to cover a surface completely with a film of liquid. It is a substance with a very low surface tension.

WHITE GLASS: Also known as milk glass, it is an opaque white glass that was originally made in Venice and meant to look like porcelain.

WROUGHT IRON: A form of iron that is relatively soft and can be bent without breaking. It contains less than 0.1% carbon.

YARN: A strand of fibers twisted together and used to make textiles.

Set Index